Why Are You Driving Me Crazy?

Why Are You Driving Me Crazy?

How the Dramas of Marriage Can
Change You for Good

Jana Edwards, LCSW

LANGDON STREET PRESS | MINNEAPOLIS, MN

Legal Disclaimer—

This publication is designed to provide accurate and authoritative information in regard to the subject matter covered. It is sold with the understanding that the publisher is not engaged in rendering psychological or other professional services. If expert assistance or counseling is needed, the services of a competent professional should be sought. To protect privacy, all patient names have been changed.

Image Credit—All figures courtesy of the author.

ISBN-13: 978-1-63505-223-7
LCCN: 2016906922

Distributed by Itasca Books

Typeset by B. Cook

Printed in the United States of America

To my brilliant and
courageous husband
who has changed me
for good.

CONTENTS

INTRODUCTION

Nature has provided us with brains that are programmed to choose a mate who will drive us crazy. There is no way to avoid this phenomenon. We go from "I'm crazy about him" when we fall in love to "I'm going to lose my mind if he doesn't stop . . . !" a few years later. Our intimate partners can make us feel crazy good and crazy bad.

The homebody marries the party guy.

The spender marries the saver.

The dyslexic marries the valedictorian.

The child of an alcoholic marries the problem drinker.

All of our brains are on a mission to express old emotions we may not even be aware are there by reliving those old emotions with someone who feels like family. Reliving happens in patterns of interaction—or dramas—dictated by the part of our brains outside of conscious awareness and repeated with frustrating consistency, until both partners feel driven crazy.

Couples who are driving each other crazy have been coming to my office for help for thirty years. The ways they are driving each other crazy range from chronic quarreling to icy distance—from abuse to boredom. Most of them have tried hard to fix their own relationships, and most of them want to save their marriages.[1] But something in each of them is driven to keep making each other feel bad the same ways over and over again, in spite of being highly capable people who are motivated to get better.

- Bill wanted everything his way, and Sally retaliated with verbal abuse.
- Katherine was reluctant to marry John because she always had to be the grown-up.
- Cynthia was tired of cleaning up the messes Matthew made with his irresponsibility.
- Both Karen and Bob were arrested for domestic violence before they came for therapy.
- Brad and Carolyn had spent thirty-six years of marriage being chronically angry at each other.
- Charles was resisting turning his live-in arrangement with Kristine into a marriage.
- Richard had been having an affair and wanted to separate from his wife, Carol.

I have devoted my career to understanding this seemingly perplexing part of human nature as I carefully observed these couples who came to me for treatment and lived through their pain with them. The names of the courageous couples you will read about in this book, as well as certain details about their lives, have been altered to protect their privacy. All of the couples have given their consent for me to use material from their treatment in this book. None of the dialogues between partners in the book are exact replications of their words said in my office, again to protect their confidentiality. However, they are representative of similar conversations that occurred during their treatment with me, some of which I observed in my office and some the couples had outside my office and subsequently reported to me in a session. Many of these conversations were much more lengthy than you will see in the book; I have included only those portions of the dialogues that I felt were necessary to adequately illustrate the concepts being demonstrated. I am immensely indebted to these couples and deeply moved that they would share their stories in the service of helping others change their lives.

INTRODUCTION

The totality of my clinical experience while treating over two hundred couples, along with my professional study of the latest developments in psychology theory and neuroscience, have brought me to a clear and hopeful vision of intimate relationships. In this book, I will share with you the scientific discoveries and my own clinical insights that explain how our brains choose the right partner to drive us crazy, why the dramas of marriage are inevitable and helpful, and how to engage in—not avoid—the stormy seas of our marriages as the best road that nature can provide us to ultimate mental health. In Part I, you will gain an understanding of exactly how and why you and your partner create together your own particular types of "crazy-making" dramas, and in Part II you will learn how to harness the constructive power of your dramas to permanently change your lives for the better.

The Science Behind *Why Are You Driving Me Crazy*

My search to unravel the mysteries of the dramas of marriage took me to the latest advances in neuroscience and theory development about the psychology of intimate relationships. If you wish to know more specifics about these scientific discoveries and the researchers and theorists who developed them, I have outlined all of the sources supporting the assertions in this book in Appendix A. Here are the scientific facts, intertwined with the knowledge and insights derived from my own experiences treating couples, that explain why it is natural for you and your partner to drive each other crazy in order to heal and grow.

The human brain is hardwired for survival.

Every neuroscientist will tell you that, from a biological perspective, our brains are constructed to make sure we stay alive long enough to reproduce.[2] Protective parts of the brain in the subcortical region that begin developing prior to birth are specifically designed to become aroused if they perceive a threat. These parts of the brain compose a *threat response network.*[3] This network includes structures and neurochemicals that send signals to various parts of the body and brain instructing them how to react to this threatening situation in order to escape harm or death. In other words, all of our brains have a built-in danger signal that goes off outside of conscious awareness if a threat is perceived.

After the present threat has passed, this potentially dangerous experience is then stored in the implicit memory within our brains—also outside of conscious awareness. This is another piece of the protective function of our brains—to store information about what we have experienced as dangerous in order to hopefully increase our chances of staying safe (and alive) in the future.

Since danger is by definition an arousing experience, the emotions connected with a potentially dangerous stimulus are stored along with any other pertinent perceptions, such as the outside source of the danger. Even if the sensed details of this arousing experience don't ever make it into explicit memory—the conscious portion of our memories—our brains will hold onto the emotional portion of the experience as essential information for survival.[4]

Dangerous emotions can make us feel "crazy."

Whether we experience a stimulus as dangerous is dependent on several factors: the age of the person having the experience, the level of harm and helplessness at the time of the experience, the potential lethality of the threat, and whether the person has been able to master this experience in the past. If we're old enough, have had the experience before, can determine that the threat isn't lethal, or have had sufficient time and help to deal with a similar experience, we might not feel it as dangerous. Obviously, children are the most vulnerable to experiencing dangerous emotions because of their underdeveloped brains, lack of experience, and level of helplessness.

Neuroscientists have labeled the two ways that we can respond to our emotions as *regulated* and *dysregulated* (simply a fancy word for "not regulated").[5] Regulated emotions are just what they sound like—under control, not upsetting, known, and safe. Dysregulated emotions don't feel under our control. They come from feeling overstimulated and overwhelmed in a way that feels unmanageable. Dysregulated emotions can feel mysterious and foreign, and the experience or source of them is usually outside our conscious awareness. They can make us overreact or completely shut down. Because dysregulated emotions maintain a sense of danger that does not permit rational functioning, I call them "crazy-making."

Infants start life experiencing almost all emotions as potentially dangerous-feeling and dysregulated. They depend on their caretakers to help them gradually learn how to regulate all normal human emotions. Researchers who study the attachment between parents and their children place great emphasis on the role of parents in helping children gradually transform their dysregulated emotions into regulated emotions.[6] Adequate parenting in this area involves providing calming and soothing when a small child becomes too disrupted by dangerous-feeling emotions. As children grow older, the regulating behaviors from their parents expand to include helping them transfer emotion-laden experiences from implicit memory (not conscious) to explicit memory (conscious) through the development of language, stories about their experiences, and modeling of ways to handle emotions. All of these steps help children learn to regulate—i.e., calm, understand, communicate, and manage—their own emotions, instead of continuing to experience them as dangerous and thereby feeling helpless to deal with them.

But there are no perfect parents. All parents have their own histories that are likely to include some experiences that have created emotions so overwhelming and overstimulating to their brains that they cannot tolerate being conscious of them. Even if they have developed some consciousness of emotionally dangerous experiences, all adults have varying degrees of tolerance for and mastery over their emotions. And in some unfortunate circumstances, the parents themselves are the source of the danger to the child. So all children grow up to be adults who have some dysregulated emotions that never make it into explicit (conscious) memory. These are our "crazy-making" feelings, and they are stored outside of our conscious awareness in what I call the nonconscious "storage bin" of the brain.[7] Roughly, this is the equivalent of our implicit memories. Our crazy-making feelings have to stay there, because we have experienced them as dangerous and, therefore, as important information for our survival.

Dangerous (dysregulated) emotions need to be *metabolized*.

Dysregulated emotions are troublemakers. They are the ones that make us feel uncomfortably stirred up, confused, or scrambled. Our hearts pound, our palms are sweaty, and we can't seem to think straight. And worst of all, our dysregulated emotions can make us do irrational things that we often later regret.

Regulating emotions requires a relational process.[8] Adequate mutual attunement between a parent and child promotes the soothing of an upset child. In a calmer state, a child's brain is able to assimilate the experience of regulation through *mirror neurons*.[9] Neuroscientists have discovered that these particular brain cells are responsible for the process that we sometimes call modeling. As one person observes another performing a certain action, the brain of the observing one is activated in exactly the same way, as if the observer is performing the same action as the person doing it. This is how children learn to copy their parents' ways of regulating their emotions.

So far, this regulating process that I am describing is happening outside of the child's conscious awareness. But in order to become a fully functioning adult whose dysregulated emotions don't cause trouble in his or her life, these emotions must move into consciousness. Implicit memories (nonconscious) must transform into explicit memories (conscious) in order to make sense of the attached emotions and constructively use them in life. Here is where science is still at work. No one has yet demonstrated neurophysiologically how this transfer happens.[10]

Enter clinical insight. During my early training as a clinician, I was taught that the struggles my patients were presenting to me largely represented "unmetabolized" emotions.[11] These are primarily the dysregulated emotions that are nonconscious and eventually need to be talked about in real time in order to heal them. I have always held onto this notion of metabolizing emotions, because it makes so much sense to me. The idea of metabolizing emotions—pieces of brain information—characterizes this process as similar to other processes within the body. Since brain and body are one, why shouldn't they be seen as processing in a similar fashion? In fact, a well-respected object relations psychoanalyst in the 1960s, Wilfred Bion, believed that this was exactly the case.[12]

Metabolism within the body is about an energy exchange that makes use of materials that have entered the system and then discards (eliminates) those which are not useful. It makes sense to me that metabolizing emotions involves an energy exchange between significant others in which the brain makes use of the information that it does need about emotions (survival and growth-enhancing information) and discards the troublemaking aspects.[13]

Metabolizing an emotion is much more than simply regulating that emotion. It is a process that requires a series of steps to fully remove the emotion from the nonconscious storage bin so that it doesn't have to be a troublemaker in your life anymore. The first step is to relive the emotion in real time in the presence of a person who is important to you. You must be consciously experiencing an unmetabolized emotion in the present to begin the metabolizing process, even if you can't clearly identify the emotion when it first shows up. Next, that important other person helps you put words to the emotion. You can't metabolize an emotion that is churning around in your own head; it has to come out of your mouth with words. I'm guessing that you have heard parents say to their toddlers, "Use your words," when those children are acting out a feeling. Language is the process through which all of us learn to understand and master our world.[14]

The next step involves validation and understanding. That important other person needs to give feedback—both verbally and with body language—that he or she has heard your emotion and has experienced it as understandable and valid. Usually this part of the process includes some form of empathy, in which you experience the other person "feeling your feelings." In addition, a conversation in which both of you talk about the past experiences that originated the emotion and the meanings attached to those experiences is necessary. However you experience the validation and understanding, you must feel known and understood by this important other person to metabolize the emotion.

The final step in the metabolizing process completes the removal of the emotion from the nonconscious storage bin in your brain, the elimination of the portions of the experience of that particular emotion that are troublemaking, and the integration of the useful parts of that old emotional experience into a more complete understanding of yourself and others.[15] The way these final processes are accomplished is through continuing conversations with that important other person in a variety of real-life circumstances that help the experience and understanding of that emotion become part of a realistic, coherent, and accepted story of your life, as well as a more complete understanding of what it means to be human. This final step is essential to the ongoing emotional growth and development of all adults.[16] You will read many of these metabolizing conversations in chapters 11 through 15.

To review, in order to metabolize an emotion, it has to be simultaneously felt and consciously known, verbally expressed with language, heard by someone who matters, and responded to in a validating manner. OK, that's all well and good, but what does it have to do with couple relationships?

INTRODUCTION

Couples are in the perfect and natural position to be each other's best healers.

I want to emphasize again that every human being has old, stored emotions that have not been metabolized prior to becoming an adult. Some natural, normal experiences in life cannot be managed by a young brain, even if a child has had the privilege of excellent parenting. The metabolizing of emotions that has not been completed during childhood will require a relationship that nonconsciously feels the same as that with the parents. Our intimate partners become that "important other person." Again, my clinical experiences over thirty years of practice have taught me that the way nature provides us with another chance at a regulating relationship is through our adult intimate partnerships. A wealth of current literature on the attachment styles of adult partners supports this statement.[17]

Having a mate is the first chance we humans have to perceive ourselves as being in the same state of vulnerability and need as we were with our parents, while also providing the safety of a potentially stable and predictable structure for getting our needs met. Our intimate partnerships provide us with the circumstances necessary to relive crazy-making feelings over and over again through repeating the same upsetting interactions with each other that have been stored in our brains since childhood. You will read about the resulting "dramas of marriage" in Part I. These dramas put intimate partners in the perfect position to potentially be each other's "mutual metabolizers."

Our brains create attraction to exactly the right partner for reliving our crazy-making feelings. This is essentially the same statement with which I started this book. Through mirror neurons, the human brain is capable, though not consciously aware, of recognizing similarity in another brain.[18] One brain becomes powerfully drawn to another brain that has similar crazy-making feelings in its nonconscious storage bin and that will be eager to re-create scenes from childhood with familiar roles being played by each intimate partner.

Mirror neurons are the neurobiological explanation for the concept that Harville Hendrix termed "imago"[19] and that Sigmund Freud and other psychodynamically oriented theorists labeled "repetition compulsion."[20] What we have learned from current research is that repeating the past with a partner who reminds us of our family of origin has a good physiological purpose. We simply cannot metabolize most of our dangerous emotions from the past without living them in the present first. And intimate partners are absolutely compelled to do this with each other—we can't *not* do it.

Rather than being seen as a negative force to be avoided, the new sciences of relationships, along with my own clinical insights, have taught me that reliving the past with our intimate partners is nature's way of giving us a chance to heal those old crazy-making feelings once and for all.[21] The steps through which you and your partner can learn to use your type of reliving to permanently rid yourselves of the past and become genuinely free to enjoy your lives together are outlined in Part II. For those who want additional practice at applying what you are discovering within these pages, I have provided exercises in Appendix B to use as you complete each chapter.

What I want you to know through reading this book:

1. Feeling driven crazy by your intimate partner is normal and unavoidable. It does not mean that you and your partner are incompatible or wrong for each other. On the contrary, it means that you are with exactly the right person for you. [While the person is always right, the timing may not be right if you and your partner can't be safe together. The issue of safety is fully covered in Part II.]

2. No matter how good you get at learning the right behaviors or communication skills to use in your marriage, your two brains

will find a way to relive any troublemaking emotions of the past that are still nonconscious and unmetabolized.

3. Feeling bored or distant in your relationship is often the outcome of attempting to avoid being driven crazy. Couples who chronically work at avoiding the crazy-making feelings that they relive together will end up with a dying relationship.

4. Research shows that people who try to avoid these crazy-making feelings by avoiding marriage get more physically ill and die younger.[22]

5. Attempting to heal your crazy-making feelings by working only on yourself might help you know yourself better, but this is only a partial solution. The most crazy-making of your feelings will be accessible *only* between you and your partner and must be addressed in that relationship in order to rid your brains of their effects.[23]

6. You can learn how to use your and your partner's crazy-making dramas to know yourself and others better than ever before and to help each other grow up into mature selves who can have a more fulfilling adult life than you previously dreamed was possible.

PART I

The Dramas of Marriage

CHAPTER 1

Characteristics of the Dramas of Marriage

Many experts who have written about the psychology of relationships have used the words "dramas" or "scripts" to describe the daily interactions that occur between family members.[1] All of us have experienced what it's like to be caught up in an emotionally charged scene with a person who is important to us. We find ourselves behaving in ways that we usually don't, we may feel like a child, and we have trouble thinking clearly. We are flooded with emotions and have an overly intense investment in how we want the "drama" to end that is often at odds with what the other person wants.

Couples develop repetitive patterns of relating to each other that simultaneously re-create in both partners the crazy-making feelings of their childhoods. These dramas of marriage are a part of nature that always occurs in intimate relationships.[2] The scenes that comprise these dramas may bear a striking similarity to actual scenes from both partners' childhoods, or they may be more creatively camouflaged. But the point is that they will cause both partners to relive precisely the emotions that are stored in their nonconscious storage bins and waiting to be metabolized.

I want to clarify why I use the word "dramas" to describe this phenomenon in marriages. (The professional literature refers to them as *enactments*.)[3] I do not intend to be derisive or comical with the use of the word drama, as in characterizing a person's behavior as "dramatic." The dramas of marriage are usually quite upsetting and painful to a couple, and they often have serious and even dangerous consequences. Sometimes the repetitive scenes of intimate relationships may not look exaggerated or overly emotional, but they always have characteristics that *feel like* a drama to the partners caught up in them. Let's look at these drama-like characteristics of the repetitive cycles of interaction in marriages.

Figure 1.1. Characteristics of marriage "dramas"

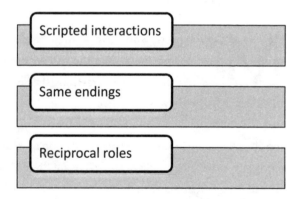

Scripted interactions

Same endings

Reciprocal roles

Scripted Interactions

Bill and Sally

The following interaction between Bill and Sally was a frequent occurrence in their marriage. Their "script" was pretty much the same every time they talked about this subject:

Bill: "Let's go up to the condo this weekend."

Sally: "I don't want to go up to the condo this weekend."

Bill: "Why not? The skiing is supposed to be great."

Sally: "We just went last weekend, I have things I need to do at home, and I don't like skiing with you."

Bill: [*reacting with hurt in his voice*] "Why don't you like skiing with me?"

Sally: "You have to go down all of the hardest runs, and it's no fun for me. I just ski for fun, not to see how many of the hardest runs I can do!"

Bill: [*pleading*] "But I really want you to ski with me."

Sally: "No! Just go without me."

Katherine and John

Katherine and John came for therapy while they were planning their wedding. They were living together and already experiencing their own particular dramas. Stopping the following type of repetitive interaction before it could ruin their new relationship was their goal.

Katherine: "Did you contact the band about booking our wedding?"

John: "No. I have plenty of time to do that."

Katherine: "But you're leaving for that assignment overseas, and you won't be back until two months before the wedding."

John: "That's plenty of time."

Katherine: "No, it isn't! I only asked you to do this one thing for the wedding *that you agreed to do, by the way,* and you can't even get that done!" [*She begins to cry.*]

John: "Why do we always have to do things your way?"

Katherine: "Because if I waited for you to get it done, it would never happen!"

Jana and Rick

And from my own marriage:

Jana: "Could you have dinner ready for us about 7:30 this evening?"

Rick:	"I think I can do that. I have a meeting that should be over about 6:00, so that'll work."
Jana:	"So, you can have it ready at 7:30?"
Rick:	"I heard you the first time. I'm not stupid, you know!"
Jana:	[*feeling somewhat horrified, hurt, and mistakenly characterized*] "I would never think that you're stupid!"

These repetitive scripts are dictated by the nonconscious storage bins of intimate partners to perfectly re-create emotions from childhood that are pressing to be metabolized. These emotions literally cannot be consciously known and metabolized until they are brought out of storage through experiencing them in the present. They cannot be talked about until they are relived.[4] Through experiences of being with each other, the brains of intimate partners learn how to use irritations and conflicts that seem to have been sparked only by present events to trigger them into a reliving drama. I have used the metaphor with my patients that the present event that begins a drama is like the starter in your car that is engaged only for a few seconds. The crazy-making feelings of the past are the engine that keeps the drama going.

The fact that these scripted interactions are momentarily triggered by the present but fueled by the unmetabolized emotions of the past leads to certain frustrations and confusion. Besides the repetitive dialogue that cannot be altered by conscious attempts to change it, the nonconscious scripts that each partner must obey have a compelling quality that can make both partners feel like they aren't being their true selves. Inside their heads, they may be thinking something like, "Why did I say that? Those words didn't feel like they came from me at all!"

The scripted interactions of the dramas of marriage cause many intimate partners to complain that their mate has changed from the person they knew during courtship or that their partner treats them differently from everyone else. They might both be thinking, "Who are you, and what have you done with the person I fell in love with?" In truth, they do act differently toward each other as the relationship develops. Their nonconscious storage bins are forcing their childhood selves to feel like they are with those important people from their pasts instead of their partner in the present.

Same Endings

Even though a couple may be trying to change the ways they relate to each other, the dramas of marriage are scripted to have the same endings every time they are replayed. It's like the needle on the phonograph record (now you know how old I am!) that gets stuck in the same place every time the song is played. In spite of consciously desiring to keep a beautiful "song" going, the nonconscious storage bins of intimate partners do a perfect job of creating dialogues that will end in both of them experiencing again and again the same crazy-making feelings that are still stored and pushing to be metabolized. The scripts end the same way every time, and both partners have the same bad feelings every time they approach the same subject.

For example, Bill and Sally repeatedly used the same behaviors they had observed in their families of origin to assert their will onto their partners. They tried again and again through coercion, emotional manipulations, intimidation, and persistent lobbying to get each other to do what they had already experienced they were not willing to do. So their scripted interactions had the same outcome every time—both of them felt unheard, disregarded, misunderstood, not cared about, and alone, just as they had in their families of origin.

Reciprocal Roles

After thirty years of treating couples, I can still be amazed at how perfectly our brains identify the right person to cast in the role of mate. In the process of getting to know each other and moving toward a committed relationship, intimate partners' nonconscious storage bins gradually experience together the roles that they will play out with each other in order to take those crazy-making feelings out of storage. It's like their storage bins "train" each other to behave in a way that will elicit the emotions they must metabolize.[5]

Almost all of these roles that our storage bins assign to our partners are a repetition of the people who were creating our emotions as children—parents, siblings, and other important caretakers. A piece of what seems like natural magic contained in human psychology is the reciprocity of these roles that we are able to perceive in a potential mate. We now know that it's probably those mirror neurons that are expediting this experience. Attraction is at its highest when two potential partners simultaneously—and mostly nonconsciously—feel like they are with someone from their families of origin who created crazy-making feelings, both good and bad.

Katherine and John were reliving roles that they had played in their families of origin. She had been what is termed a "parentified child"[6] who had been compelled to act too mature for her age and to take care of many of her parents' needs that they should have been getting met by others. John had been permitted by parents who were rather lax in their disciplining to continue being childlike into his adulthood. So Katherine continued to do a lot more caretaking than being taken care of, and John's immaturity deprived him of the experience of feeling good about himself as a competent adult.

In the above example from my own marriage, this type of repetitive interaction arose from perfectly complementary reciprocal roles that simultaneously elicited stored emotions from both of our childhoods. In my family of origin, people really weren't listening to me, leaving me with a reservoir of emotions about my stories not being important to the folks I depended on the most to know and understand me. I could count on the fact that they would not remember what I had told them, particularly if it was in the context of asking for a need of my own to be met. At the same moment, my need to repeat myself in order to be heard caused my husband to experience again the emotions he had as a child about having undiagnosed learning disabilities and being treated as if he were stupid. It was the "perfect storm" for both of our feelings to be taken out of storage in a present moment.

So how do our brains get attracted to the right person for reliving the past? How do they "know" who to cast in the role of mate for creating these dramas of marriage?

CHAPTER 2

The Brain as Casting Director

Our brains begin accumulating data about the type of person we will cast in the role of mate before we are even born.[1] A mother's body rhythms—her heartbeat, voice, and respirations—provide the regulated structure that organizes the development of the baby's brain in the womb and creates the foundation of the baby's attachment to the mother. After birth, the brains of infants can form new learning connections at the amazingly rapid rate of three billion per second.[2] A sizable portion of the data infants' brains are recording are experiences with their significant caretakers who are teaching them about relationships and how those relationships cause them to feel about themselves and others.

With my patients, I have likened the developing brain of a child to the hard disk on a computer. The vast majority of the data that most significantly affects how we see ourselves and others is recorded on the disc by the time we are six years old. All relationship experiences after that age are like the "software" of life, and those experiences will be related to the information that our brains have already stored about ourselves and others. Traumatic experiences[3] and consistent, conscious work are primarily the only ways the disc can be changed after that time.

Our brains create a *relationship template* composed of the relationship experiences that we had during those first six years of our lives. The relationship template contains the conclusions that we came to about ourselves and about how to connect to significant others as a result of the daily process of trying to get our needs met from them. And it contains the most important criteria our brains will use to act as casting director for the perfect intimate partner for each of us. Let's look more closely at what makes up the relationship template.

Figure 2.1. Relationship template

How We Know Ourselves

Psychologists name all of the mental, emotional, physical, and spiritual ways in which our brains have stored information about ourselves the *sense of self*.[4] It is obvious that the experiences we have in our families of origin are extremely important and powerful in the development of a sense of self. A person's sense of self has been organized around experiences with his or her family in early childhood, and we will reference all later experiences back to that sense of self.[5] The most important aspects of the sense of self are all the ways we have learned to feel loved, loving, valuable, powerful, competent, and needed.

Interactional patterns within families that cause children to feel loved, loving, valuable, powerful, competent, and needed in ways that are *not* good for them often lead to a distorted, unhealthy, and dysfunctional sense of self. But patterns that seemed to work in the family of origin become an important aspect of the self—an integral component of self-esteem. For example, if you had an alcoholic father who praised you for hiding his drinking from your mother, you will have learned to feel proud of yourself for being a good liar. Or maybe you have parents who got divorced and never allowed you or anyone else to talk about how bad it felt. You have developed the ability to show the world-class stiff upper lip, no matter how you really feel, and you brag that nothing ever gets to you.

Bill and Sally's marital dramas demonstrated that they had similar self-experiences: "If I really want to do something, I'll just have to do it by myself." Katherine was the caretaker and John the caretakee in their relationship. Part of my relationship template was experiencing myself as unimportant, and my husband had stored many self-experiences that led to a belief that he was woefully inadequate.

How We Know Ourselves with Others

Our relationships to significant others are the primary constructors of the relationship template. Therefore, our sense of self is almost wholly constructed in the process of interacting with our families during childhood.[6] They show us who we are by the way they respond to us and get us to respond to them from the first day of life. We learn the aspects of ourselves that get rewarded and those that make our significant others anxious, angry, sad, mean, unsafe, and so forth. We learn to be adept at the behaviors they like and to eliminate the behaviors they don't. Birth order and number of siblings are significant contributors to how we know ourselves with others. The roles that all family members are assigned within the family, particularly in regard to power and how everyone gets what they need and want, are also major factors in the development of this portion of the template.

A critically important aspect of this portion of the relationship template comes from both implicit and explicit childhood memories around how our significant caretakers responded when we did something "bad." Children need to be taught how to contain themselves, how to treat others with care and respect, and how to grow into productive adults. They will inevitably have to experience disapproval at some point in their young lives, and they will have to experience the shameful feelings that go along with that disapproval. What gets recorded in their relationship templates is which behaviors lead to feeling shame, how committed their parents are to making them emotionally suffer for being "bad," and how quickly and safely they get rescued from their shameful feelings. I will elaborate further on the importance of the experience of shame within our relationship templates in chapter 6.

This leads me to that portion of our relationship templates that tells us how safe it feels to be close to the people we need the most.[7] As children we learn quickly how close we can risk being to our family members without fear of being criticized, rejected, hurt, harmed, and/or shamed.[8] Recorded within our nonconscious storage bins are the emotions that dictate the precise balance of closeness and distance we must maintain in any of our intimate relationships in order to feel safe—not too close and not too far. These closeness/distance "rules" become a highly significant and powerful portion of the relationship template.

Intimate partners will often assume opposite-looking roles to maintain the balance of closeness and distance that both must experience—the proverbial pursuer and pursued. If one partner moves in too close, the other will create distance. If one partner creates distance, the other will do something to reestablish the original level of closeness that their storage bins have dictated as comfortable. One partner may look like the agent of closeness and the other the agent of distance, but their nonconscious patterns dictate that the relationship must always maintain the balance of distance and closeness both partners need to stay safe in an intimate relationship.

Marital dramas that require specific barriers to closeness are a frequent manifestation of both partners coming from families that fostered significant fears of intimacy. Couples whose work schedules keep them apart, who don't live together, who live together or have children together without marrying, or whose ages are far enough apart not to be in the same developmental stage are demonstrating the need to reexperience extra barriers to closeness. Addictions, different religions or cultures, and overinvolvement with children or families of origin can also be barriers. Couples with these external and concrete types of barriers have mutually interlocking relationship templates that were likely nonconsciously constructed to avoid the crazy-making feelings associated with the intrinsic inability or unwillingness of their parents to be safely close to them and to meet their dependency needs.

Crazy-making Feelings

Crazy-making feelings are the emotions I described in the introductory chapter that are dysregulated and unmetabolized. They are stored in our nonconscious storage bins because they are attached to danger. They are disruptive and overwhelming, and therefore capable of making us feel "crazy."

We depend on our closest relationships to help us manage emotions when we are children. We look to our families to help us regulate ourselves when we are having experiences that lead to emotions that overwhelm our brains. Caretakers respond to emotions that could be dysregulating to children on a continuum from support and comfort to anger, punishment, and withdrawal. The support and comfort response helps children gradually know that they are going to be OK and learn how to put words to what they are feeling. So the ways our parents respond to our emotions become part of our relationship templates.[9] Obviously, some families are better at this than others. Parents who have not learned themselves how to master their own crazy-making feelings will likely leave their children with a large store of unmetabolized crazy-making feelings in this part of their relationship templates. But I will emphasize once again that even the best parenting cannot adequately protect a child's brain from needing to store some unmetabolized emotions.

I mentioned in the first paragraph of this book that our intimate relationships can make us feel crazy good. That "falling in love" feeling can dysregulate our lives—we can't sleep as well as we used to; our appetites decrease; we think obsessively about the one we love. This extremely pleasurable crazy-making feeling is a reliving of the *ecstasy* that starts the process of infants knowing themselves with their mothers. Infants are ready, willing, and able to connect to their mothers in as many ways and as deeply as the mother will allow, and the endorphins released during this experience of oneness between infant and mother create a sensation in the child of being totally filled up with well-being and erotic pleasure. This ecstasy that both baby and mother can feel in the interchanges between them becomes a powerful part of our sexuality and our relationship templates.[10] Those who have experienced baby/mother ecstasy want it again; those who were unlucky enough not to experience it want another chance to have it. The continual and compelling pursuit of these crazy good feelings leads to some of the crazy bad feelings in our relationship templates.

The chart below lists the primary categories of crazy bad feelings I have seen most often manifest in the dramas of marriage. You will notice that each category of emotion shows a progression from a feeling in its most familiar and more manageable state to its more primitive and threatening ("crazy-making") state, shown in capital letters.[11]

While couples will sometimes have some conscious awareness of the less threatening emotion triggering a drama, their reliving of a script is intended to get at the more nonconscious and dangerous form of the emotion. The more threatening form of the emotion is deeply disturbing, even to an adult brain. It has sometimes been originally generated by a traumatic experience or traumatic pattern of relating[12] that is so difficult for even a grown-up to deal with that it must be symbolically and secretly encased in a marital drama.[13]

Figure 2.2. Unmetabolized emotions commonly relived in marriages

Fear→TERROR
Anger→RAGE
Hurt→ANNIHILATION
Loneliness→ABANDONMENT
Inadequacy→SHAME
Helplessness→DESPAIR
Sadness→SORROW

From top to bottom on this chart, the unmetabolized emotions increase in difficulty from the easiest to access to the hardest to access. The farther down the chart one goes, the more the emotions represent increasing levels of vulnerability in coping with our natural human condition and therefore an increasing likelihood that they will be stored and unmetabolized. In the chapters that follow, you will see how these crazy-making feelings get experienced by couples as their brains co-construct their own particular type of dramas. In Part II, I will elaborate on the exact nature of each of these categories of unmetabolized emotions. But first we will look at how they appear in the dramas of marriage and how the brains of intimate partners "know" that they have the same emotions waiting to be metabolized. The "casting" of the reciprocal roles necessary to experience their dramas is accomplished by both brains being attracted to a matching relationship template.

Matching Relationship Templates

Treating couples has taught me that the biological drive to mate in adulthood is the moment that the human brain perceives as the perfect opportunity to metabolize all of those stored crazy-making feelings. The experience of falling in love happens when the nonconscious storage bins in potential partners' minds become excited that they have found exactly the right candidate for specifically and literally reliving all of their old unmetabolized emotions.[14] People certainly have conscious reasons to fall in love—commonalities of interests, values, and goals among the most important. But the matching of nonconscious aims within the psychologies of intimate partners is far more compelling than the conscious ones. Many candidates for mates are attractive and we might feel pleasurable familiarity with them, but the few with whom we have "chemistry" are the ones whose relationship templates match our own.

Although on its face reliving all of our most painful experiences from the past seems self-destructive, this is the only way the human brain can create an opportunity to metabolize those stored crazy-making feelings. We must be experiencing the same emotion at the same level of intensity in conscious awareness to set the stage for it to be effectively taken out of storage and thoroughly metabolized. So the critical element our brains seek when casting the role of mate is that being in a relationship with them creates all of the same crazy-making feelings that we had as children. The subjective matching of emotional pain from the past is an amazing and seemingly magical piece of how our brains find a mate. Through mirror neurons, the storage bins in the brains of potential partners "recognize" each other's past experiences.[15] Their pain may be about different events and may have come about in different ways, but it was *subjectively experienced* during childhood by both members of the couple as exactly the same. I have often described this to couples as having matching "scars around their hearts."

Sometimes their stories are eerily similar. In one couple I treated, both of their fathers had crashed airplanes they were piloting. In the wife's case, the crash occurred before she was born, and her father never fully recovered from the experience. The husband's father died in his crash when my patient was only six years old. Sometimes a couple is conscious of their matching pain from the beginning of the relationship. In this case, they have probably been able to openly share their common experiences and to empathize with each other. This type of shared pain has probably been felt as a contributor to their closeness all along, and it is not a source of trouble in the marriage. But *nonconscious* matching pain comes from those crazy-making feelings that must be repeated by intimate partners in the present.

Besides the matching of crazy-making feelings, potential partners have experiences as they get to know each other that satisfy the requirements for those reciprocal roles that must be played out to relive their unmetabolized emotions. They act out familiar parts that are either the same or complementary in an interlocking pattern of relating that gradually re-creates the dramas necessary to offer opportunities for emptying their nonconscious storage bins.[16] Although we often experience this naturally human process as some form of torturing each other, it is perfectly designed to be the only route to eventual freedom from the past.

17

Let's take a look at how all of the elements of the matching relationship templates came together in the marriages you've read about so far.

Figure 2.3. Matching relationship template of Bill and Sally

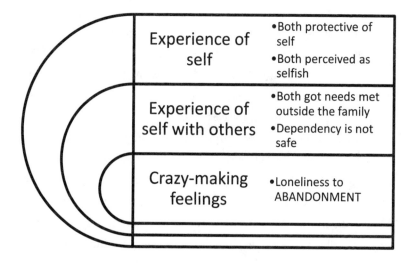

Experience of self	•Both protective of self •Both perceived as selfish
Experience of self with others	•Both got needs met outside the family •Dependency is not safe
Crazy-making feelings	•Loneliness to ABANDONMENT

Both Bill and Sally had been psychologically and emotionally abandoned children. All of their parents were so developmentally immature themselves that they could not attend to their children's needs. Sally and Bill were repeating this experience of emotional abandonment with each other, as they both felt victimized by their partner's callous disregard for their feelings and needs. Their mutual need to feel loved and valued by each other was buried beneath years of hurtful interactions in which neither of them got what they needed from each other and both felt that their only choice was to be alone. They were both aware of feeling lonely, but the full extent of the abandonment they both felt as children was still in their nonconscious storage bins.

Even though Katherine was originally attracted to the fun-loving and easygoing aspect of John, she was getting tired of having to be the grown-up in their relationship. The pseudomaturity that her family of origin had required of her as a child had robbed her of the only truly carefree years

Figure 2.4. Matching relationship template of Katherine and John

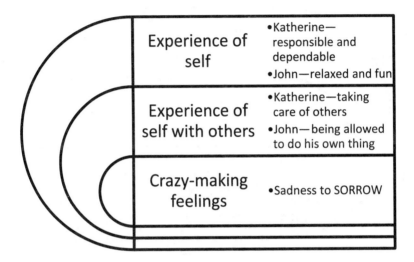

Experience of self	•Katherine— responsible and dependable •John—relaxed and fun
Experience of self with others	•Katherine—taking care of others •John—being allowed to do his own thing
Crazy-making feelings	•Sadness to SORROW

that a human being can have. The lack of appropriate discipline that John's laissez-faire parents had demonstrated had robbed him of what he needed to truly enjoy his adulthood as a dependable and competent man. The deep sorrow that both John and Katherine were nonconsciously tapping into about their childhood losses was being camouflaged beneath their dramas of arguing over John's irresponsibility.

My husband and I had no inherent inadequacies as children. But our experiences with significant others in our lives convinced us that we had, so our matching nonconscious storage bins contained a lot of unmetabolized shame. In the scripted interaction between us that you read above, we could both relive shame by inadvertently wounding each other while simultaneously feeling wounded. Each of our nonconscious storage bins acted out of a sense of each other as being exactly like the people we grew up with, thereby exposing our old unmetabolized emotions in the rawness of present hurt and shame.

Figure 2.5. **Matching relationship template in my marriage**

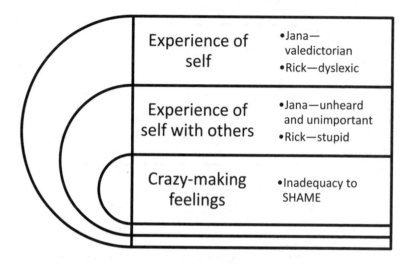

These examples illustrate how our brains choose partners who fulfill the requirements for the reciprocal roles that are dictated in the first two parts of the relationship template in order to relive the matching crazy-making feelings of the third part. I have described above one particular emotion in each couple that is being relived in one particular drama. But obviously couples can experience several repetitive dramas about many emotions. In the next four chapters, we will look at how all of these elements of the matching relationship templates of intimate partners come together to create the most common forms of marital dramas. In hopes of more clearly demonstrating the unmetabolized emotions relived in each type of drama, I have chosen couples whose stories may seem to be on a more exaggerated and highly conflictual end of a continuum. Nevertheless, dramas that appear less filled with conflict or trauma are fulfilling the same purposes in the marital relationship that are described in each chapter.

CHAPTER 3

Dramas of Opposites

Cynthia and Matthew

Cynthia: "We just got a notice from our mortgage company that we are behind on our payments. You told me that you would take over paying the mortgage."

Matthew: "Oh, no! I forgot to send it in."

Cynthia: [*with great dismay and disgust*] "I can't believe you forgot! You promised that you would take care of this! What if we lose the house?"

Matthew: "I'm sorry; I just forgot. What is wrong with me?"

Cynthia: "How could you be so irresponsible? Do I have to do EVERYTHING?"

When this couple came for therapy they were on the verge of divorce, and it was not the first time they had been there. They were both approaching fifty years of age. They had been married almost twenty years and had two teenage children. Both Matthew and his thirteen-year-old son had been diagnosed and medicated for mood disorders. The recurrent dramas in the marriage were fueled by Cynthia's fury toward her husband for being incompetent at the practicalities of life. Her experience was that she could not count on him to take care of business, and that she—by default—ended up being the one to clean up his messes.

Reciprocal Roles of Cynthia and Matthew

It was readily apparent in this couple that they were both repeating the roles they had been nonconsciously assigned in their families of origin. Cynthia appeared highly competent, organized, dependable, and responsible. As the oldest child, she was forced to be the "adult" in her family, because neither of her parents could be. They both looked to her to solve problems in the family that should not have been hers to solve. She was accustomed to that job, and she did it quite well. It had become an important part of her self-concept and self-esteem to see herself as better than other people at all of those things she was required to do in her family of origin and to be certain that she knew the "right" way to handle life.

Matthew's matching relationship template was more than eager to oblige her need to be the competent one, as he continued the role he had played in his family as well. Although he was the oldest child and destined to follow in his father's footsteps as a physician, his sister was perceived as the competent child. Matthew was derided and ridiculed by his family as being disorganized and goofy. He was never permitted to compete with his father in any way—father was definitively and clearly "king of the hill."

Crazy-making Feelings of Cynthia and Matthew

The polar opposite roles in this marriage created dramas in which one partner could consciously experience and express emotions that the other was keeping completely out of conscious awareness. But both could think that these feelings were being generated in the present by each

Figure 3.1. Matching relationship template of Cynthia and Matthew

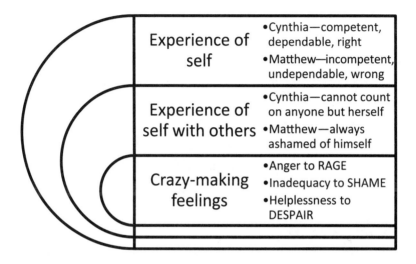

Experience of self	•Cynthia—competent, dependable, right •Matthew—incompetent, undependable, wrong
Experience of self with others	•Cynthia—cannot count on anyone but herself •Matthew—always ashamed of himself
Crazy-making feelings	•Anger to RAGE •Inadequacy to SHAME •Helplessness to DESPAIR

other's behavior. Cynthia felt justified in her righteously punitive attitude toward Matthew, because she felt like the victim of his irresponsible behavior. She truly *was* the victim of her *parents'* irresponsible behavior. In her family of origin she did have to do "everything." Most of her anger at her husband was fueled by unmetabolized rage at her parents. Rage is the natural human response to having our need-meeting behaviors blocked or our well-being threatened. Matthew's rage at having been truly victimized by his parents was even further buried into his nonconscious storage bin than was Cynthia's. He went along with being the object of *her* rage in order to completely camouflage his own crazy-making rage and keep it out of conscious awareness.

At the same time that Cynthia was consciously experiencing anger at her husband, he was consciously feeling inadequate. I don't think that Cynthia had ever been consciously aware of feeling inadequate. Matthew was painfully familiar with being shamed in his family of origin, but Cynthia would have said that everyone in her family except her should be ashamed of themselves. She had no mastery of the normal human emotion of shame, and he had no mastery of the normal human emotion of rage, so their brains had to try to get those crazy-making feelings into conscious awareness by watching each other play them out.

The emotion they both were aware of feeling was helplessness to get what they needed from each other. They shared a lack of conscious awareness that their dramas of opposites were replaying the deep despair they both had experienced as children about ever getting what they needed from their parents. Despair is about hopelessness—an emotion that is too life-threatening to a small child's brain and must be sent to the nonconscious storage bin and saved for later metabolizing.

Dramas of Opposites
Opposites do attract. This phenomenon in nature is one with which most people are familiar. The extrovert pairs up with the introvert; the saver marries a spender; the aggressive person chooses a passive one. Most of us have had experiences in our lives or observed others in which the rule of opposites attracting is quite clear.[1]

Conscious pairing of opposites is likely to be known from the beginning of a relationship and is often experienced as a pleasurable asset to each partner's life. Aspects of functioning that one partner doesn't enjoy or isn't good at can be supplied by the other partner, creating a type of external balancing in the relationship that both consciously appreciate.

On the other hand, the matching relationship templates of intimate partners often create dramas about experiencing each other as opposites in ways they *dislike* to circumvent conscious awareness of unmetabolized crazy-making feelings in *both* partners.[2] When couples are reliving a drama about being opposites, their brains are attempting to "kill two birds with one stone." One partner is openly expressing an emotion that both need to experience and metabolize. They are reliving in the present a matching crazy-making feeling that is attempting to move out of storage.[3] But at the same time, this emotion is being perceived as so problematic to the current relationship that it reinforces to both brains that it is too dangerous to metabolize and must be recycled back into storage.

The side that one partner takes represents an emotion that is nonconsciously disowned by the other partner, in other words not felt or experienced.[4] The disowning of particular emotions becomes part of the relationship template through experiences in our families of origin that the expressions of these emotions cannot be tolerated and must be devalued. We learn from repeated interactions in our families—directly or by inference, consciously or nonconsciously, by what they actually did or said or by our own creation of meaning—that the disowned emotion is the wrong way to feel.[5] Marital dramas about opposite characteristics reinforce that our families of origin were correct in teaching us to disown certain crazy-making feelings. So the dramas of opposites lead to couples driving each other crazy and recycling those matching crazy-making feelings back into their nonconscious storage bins.

CHAPTER 4

Competition Dramas

Karen and Bob

[*On a hike*]

Karen: [*pointing to one side of a fork in a trail*] "I think that we're supposed to go this way."

Bob: "No, that's the wrong way. We go this way." [*pointing to the other side*]

Karen: "No; you're not looking at the map the right way. The trail goes this way."

Bob: "Yes, I *am* looking at it the right way, but once again, you're convinced that I'm wrong!"

Karen: "Can't we just have a nice hike without getting into an argument every time?"

Bob: "I *was* having a nice hike, but now you've ruined it! I'm going back to the car!"

[*Playing Scrabble together*]

Bob: "That's not a real word that you just put down."

Karen: "Yes, it is."

Bob: "Well, let's look it up. I'll bet it's not."

Karen: "Are you accusing me of cheating?"

Bob: "No, but look; it's not a real word."

Karen: "Just forget it. I don't want to play anymore!"

This couple could fight over anything, so their arguments were frequent and often nasty. During their disagreements, Karen and Bob experienced each other the same way—as irrational, controlling, and demanding to have things their own way. They were compelled to vehemently, righteously, and emotionally establish who was right and who was wrong and therefore who deserved to get what he or she wanted and who did not.

A few weeks before they started treatment with me, their mutual compulsion to determine which one of them was the worst person resulted in an argument that escalated into getting physical with each other. In spite of their hope that the police would establish which one of them was innocent, to their surprise and horror, both of them were arrested, incarcerated, and sentenced for domestic violence. They were each beginning attendance at their own separate mandatory thirty-six-week group treatment, but amazingly they were so invested in saving their marriage that they also decided to come for marital therapy.

Bob and Karen had met each other in college, and they both described their courtship as filled with positive feelings and experiences. She described the first ten years of their marriage as good but busy with getting Bob's career as a sales rep off and running. They had their two sons, and Karen worked in the computer industry sometimes full time and sometimes part time.

In the second decade of the marriage, all hell broke loose. Bob was exhibiting behavior patterns which indicated to Karen that he was suffering from a clinical depression, and he was periodically abusing alcohol. While he made some attempts at getting treatment, he had difficulty staying consistent with either medications or therapy. Bob's work became increasingly stressful and unfulfilling. By the time they got to my office after twenty years of marriage, they had built up mountains of hostile and hurt feelings toward each other, and every disagreement between them resulted in a nasty argument and no resolution.

This couple had the deck stacked against them in terms of family histories. Both of their childhoods were filled with trauma. When he was four years old, Bob's mother suddenly and secretly left his father, literally kidnapping Bob. She took Bob with her out of the country but left Bob's younger sister behind, saying that she "just didn't want her"! Bob had no contact with his father or his sister for most of his childhood. His mother remarried an authoritarian and controlling man who related to Bob with little warmth and understanding. Bob's mother died when he was seventeen years old, and his stepfather abandoned him to fend for himself.

Karen's family stayed together, but it was a hellish home. Her father was chronically abusive in every way except sexual. He literally terrorized his wife and children on a regular basis with threats to kill one or all of them if they did not respond completely to his control. Karen often took on a protective role toward her mother and siblings, and they all supported the notion that it was impossible for their mother to leave the marriage. Her parents stayed married, and the dynamics in the relationships among the members of her family of origin never changed.

At the beginning of treatment, Karen was more conscious than Bob of how awful her childhood had been. She had never denied to herself that her father had tortured everyone in the family with his sadistic and horribly dangerous behaviors. On the other hand, Bob had idealized his mother and convinced himself that he did not have much attachment to his biological father. He reserved his only conscious awareness of parenting deficiencies for his stepfather, whom he intensely disliked.

Reciprocal Roles of Karen and Bob

Both Karen and Bob had been perceived as the good children in their families of origin. As the oldest, Karen had become a protector for her siblings and her mother. She was not afraid to stand up to her abusive father. Bob's mother had dramatically and pathologically demonstrated that he was her chosen child. Although his father claimed to have made repeated attempts to find his son, Bob saw him as pretty powerless and ineffectual. So both of their family systems had contained one parent who appeared like the good, innocent, but weak one (Karen's mother and Bob's father) and the other was the bad, selfish, but powerful one (Karen's father and Bob's mother).

Figure 4.1. Matching relationship template of Karen and Bob

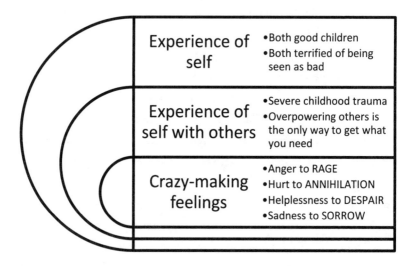

Experience of self	•Both good children •Both terrified of being seen as bad
Experience of self with others	•Severe childhood trauma •Overpowering others is the only way to get what you need
Crazy-making feelings	•Anger to RAGE •Hurt to ANNIHILATION •Helplessness to DESPAIR •Sadness to SORROW

The marital dramas that came out of Bob and Karen's matching relationship template demonstrated how determined they both were to never be perceived as "the bad guy." They both went to great lengths to prove that they deserved to have what they wanted and needed because they had earned it by being good. When they remembered or perceived events from their lives differently, they could argue endlessly about who was right and who was wrong. They then felt enraged at each other for being wrongly characterized and deprived of whatever they had determined each rightfully deserved.

Crazy-making Feelings of Karen and Bob

The anger that fueled Bob and Karen's disputes was a clear reliving of the rage that they rightfully felt for being maltreated children. Everyone in their families of origin had been powerless to stop the destruction of the self-centered and dangerous parents. These types of parents send a message to their children that they are never safe, that the needs and well-being of others mean nothing, and that the potential to be emotionally—or even physically—destroyed is real. What Karen and Bob had both experienced in childhood was failure to escape the effects of the "badness" in her father and his mother. Even though Bob and Karen loved each other and wished to treat each other much better than their parents had done, the psychological bottom line in both of them was, "I will protect myself at all costs, even if it means hurting you." They were reliving their matching childhood pain in repetitive dramas in which they located the badness within their partner and recycled feeling unknown and alone.

Both Bob and Karen felt compelled to let the passive parent off the hook. Bob wanted to see his father, and Karen wanted to see her mother as helpless, innocent victims—the "all good" people—who had no choice but to go along with the villains. Karen and Bob identified with their "innocent" parents, as they both continued to feel helpless to get what they needed from each other. Their desperation to have an impact on each other had culminated in the horrifying domestic violence experience that had propelled them into couples treatment. All the despair they both felt about being abandoned by the parents who stood by and let them get hurt was still stored away.

Bob and Karen were recycling the unmetabolized crazy-making feelings of their childhoods by seeing *each other* as the abandoner and perpetrator, rather than knowing that the genuine sources of the majority of their pain were their families of origin. They were aware of feeling sad about the deterioration of their marriage, but they had no idea about the depth of their sorrow around their parents having effectively ruined their childhoods. Both thought they had successfully and magically escaped that sorrow by creating a new family in which they had all of the power to keep that awful stuff from happening again. But their nonconscious storage bins had compelled them into competition dramas in order to experience all of these crazy-making feelings in the present.

Dramas about Competition
Everybody wants to be loved by their parents. We all look to them when we are children to know whether we can perceive ourselves as valuable and lovable or not. Our experiences in this aspect of self comprise a significant portion of our relationship templates. We cannot know when we are little that getting loved by our parents is purely based on *their* abilities to love— not on any question about whether we are inherently lovable. It takes a certain level of developmental maturity to have the capacity to love, and parents who have not reached that level cannot love their children unconditionally. They will send a message to their children that their love is conditional on those children performing a certain way for the parents.

It is natural for children to feel competitive with their siblings and sometimes even with one or both parents. In families with parents who developmentally have the capacity to love, this competitiveness is minimized, and the children have the experience of being equally loved for simply being their natural selves. In families with parents whose developmental immaturity leads them to love conditionally, this competitive atmosphere is heightened. Their children vie for the coveted position of being the good child, the one that makes the parents proud with his or her accomplishments, the one whose behavior is held up as the right way to act. The crazy-making feelings that these children must store are all of the ones that would be unacceptable to the parents—that would get them told their feelings are wrong or that feeling that way makes them bad people.

Couples whose repetitive dramas are about competition have matching stored emotions about not having been unconditionally loved in their families of origin. They argue about whose emotions are justified, and they require proof about whether they should be accused of inflicting pain on the other. They behave as if it is impossible for both of them to get what they need in the relationship, and they keep score about which of them has earned getting what he or she wants. Above all, these couples are recycling their unmetabolized crazy-making feelings by blaming each other for all of those bad feelings that their parents originally created. Seeing their parents as the sources of their unacceptable emotions would cause them to lose the competition in their families for who has the right to be loved.

CHAPTER 5

Victims and Villains Dramas

Brad and Carolyn

[*Carolyn walks into the dining room as Brad is setting the table for a family dinner they're hosting.*]

Carolyn: "Oh. I was thinking of using a different table setting this time."

Brad: [*with frustration and some irritation in his voice*] "So, I did it wrong."

Carolyn: "I didn't say you did it wrong. I just wish you had asked me what I had in mind before you did it."

Brad: [*now feeling angry and hurt*] "You don't think I know how to set a table? I guess I just shouldn't have tried to be helpful!"

Carolyn: "I didn't say that either. But you don't ever care about what I want before you just go ahead and do something."

Brad: [*now shouting at Carolyn*] "You're right! I don't care! I don't ever care!"

[*Brad angrily stomps out and prepares to leave the house.*]

Carolyn: "Where are you going? Our kids will be here for dinner any minute! When will you be back?"

Brad: "I don't know!"

Victims and Villains Dramas

Couples who are in pain often need to portray themselves as the victims and their partners as the villains.[1] A large majority of the couples I see enter treatment with a figurative or literal finger pointed at their partners, in essence saying, "Make him or her stop arguing with me; belittling me; abusing me; hurting me; cheating on me; letting me down; etc., etc., etc." They are hoping that I will agree to act as judge and jury, protecting the (obviously) innocent one and correcting the (obviously) guilty one.

The purest form of victim is a child. Children have no choice about many important aspects of their lives and only as much power as their parents allow them to have. If they do not have emotionally healthy and developmentally mature parents, they get victimized by their *parents'* marital dramas. This parental victimizing then becomes part of the relationship template which must be relived by a couple in order for both partners to access the crazy-making feelings they both had in childhood.

This drama from the past that is being relived by a couple requires that the "victim" experience having no power over being victimized and no power to make it stop. One partner feels something like, "I did absolutely nothing to warrant being treated badly by you, and I can do absolutely nothing to get out of this bad situation." The partner playing the "villain" feels strangely compelled to behave in bad or mean ways that sometimes seem foreign to his or her previous sense of self. And to further complicate this scenario, the "villain" will claim that he or she is being victimized by the "victim." So the scripted interactions of this type of marital drama lead both partners to experience the crazy-making helplessness of victims while simultaneously being characterized as the one who is causing all of the other harming emotions of the villain.[2]

The enactment of victims and villains dramas precludes being an adult. Having no power means also having no responsibility. Playing the role of the helpless child relieves a marital partner from taking responsibility for his or her own needs, preferences, behaviors, and emotions. It transfers accountability for what is happening within the relationship from one partner to the other, and it always blocks the path to metabolizing crazy-making feelings from the past by maintaining the childhood role of victim. Staying in childhood roles allows us to believe that we can redo our childhoods, instead of relinquishing that belief and dealing with the real childhood we had.

This type of marital drama is the perfect venue for experiencing in the present all of the crazy-making feelings each partner stored in childhood: anger at the villain, fear of abandonment, the hurt and helplessness of the victim, the shame of both victim and villain, and eventual sadness if the marriage ends. The intensity of the current victim and villain interactions makes it seem so obvious to each player in the drama that their emotions should be assigned to the present instead of the past. Nobody wants to believe that they were victimized by their own parents, so the couple keeps doing it to each other.

The victims and villains dramas are a particular type of competition about which partner is the "bad" one. Affairs and domestic violence are examples of these types of dramas in which society at large gets involved in assigning total blame to one partner and total innocence to the other. These dramas cause a great deal of pain in the present lives of marital partners and aptly demonstrate the tremendous power that the matching relationship templates can exert to force people into roles that they would never consciously choose.

Reciprocal Roles of Brad and Carolyn

Brad and Carolyn grew up in the same small Midwestern town, but they didn't start dating until they were in college. Carolyn saw Brad as the BMOC she would have never expected to attract—not surprising for a woman who felt chronically unworthy of love. After they married, Brad immersed himself in beginning his career with a large banking organization, and Carolyn felt left to primarily raise their two children alone.

About fifteen years into their marriage, Brad began having an affair with a coworker, thereby fully assuming his role as the "villain" in the marital dramas. He and Carolyn went through a few years of painful struggles about his affair, including separations and both individual and couples therapy (with another therapist). Although Brad eventually decided to stay in the marriage, Carolyn never believed that he fully understood the suffering she had gone through during all of these years in their relationship.

It was inevitable that this couple would be compelled to enact victims and villains dramas, because both of them had been genuine victims in childhood. Brad's mother appeared to have an undiagnosed and untreated mental illness which manifested in dramatic mood swings and emotional meltdowns over simple perceived slights toward her. There was an obsessive-compulsive quality to much of her behavior, as is often the case in people who experience normal life as unbearably anxiety provoking. She frequently accused Brad of intentionally hurting her if he inadvertently upset her "program," and he learned to escape her tirades by jumping on his bicycle and riding away from her. You saw in the scripted interaction above how this childhood pattern was being almost exactly repeated with his wife.

Of course, Carolyn's reciprocal role was a reliving of her childhood as well. As the oldest child in her family of origin, she had been forced into service as a "little mother" because her own mother wasn't interested in meeting the needs of her three children. Tragically, the neglect of her mother and absence of her busy father had resulted in episodes of Carolyn being victimized sexually by more than one male in her small hometown. She truly was not adequately nurtured and protected by her parents, leading to her own understandable conclusion that she was not lovable. Thus, the stage was set for the recurring dramas in this marriage in which Carolyn could look like the obvious victim of Brad's "bad" behavior, and he could continue feeling like the villain who hurt those he was supposed to love.

Figure 5.1. Matching relationship template of Brad and Carolyn

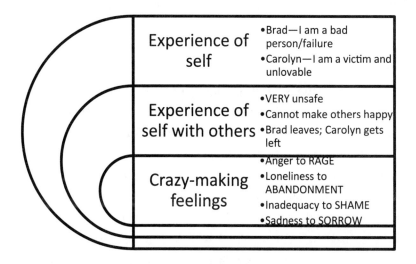

Experience of self	•Brad—I am a bad person/failure •Carolyn—I am a victim and unlovable
Experience of self with others	•VERY unsafe •Cannot make others happy •Brad leaves; Carolyn gets left
Crazy-making feelings	•Anger to RAGE •Loneliness to ABANDONMENT •Inadequacy to SHAME •Sadness to SORROW

In the marital dramas of Carolyn and Brad, the role of "bad guy" had been nonconsciously assigned to Brad. They could endlessly fight about what he had done to Carolyn, instead of being conscious of all of the pain surrounding the ways they had been emotionally abandoned by all of their parents. Carolyn could continue believing that her husband didn't love her instead of dealing with having unloving parents. Brad could continue to see himself as a hurtful person, since that's exactly what his mother had told him he was.

Crazy-making Feelings of Brad and Carolyn

When Carolyn and Brad started couples treatment with me, she stated that she could not stop being openly angry at him. She couldn't get past the suffering she had endured during Brad's affair and uncertainties about continuing their marriage, and she felt compelled to reassert her position as the victim whenever something brought up her feelings about being unworthy of Brad's love. Then she would relive all of her feelings about having been the true victim of sexual assaults as a child, complete with the usual shame of abuse victims that accompanies their belief that they did something to invite or provoke the assault.

Their joint experience of his psychology was that he did not know how to access his emotions and, therefore, could not enter into the mutual conversations about feelings that Carolyn wanted him to have with her. His state of mind at that time was that he deserved her anger, as he consciously felt ashamed for all he had put her through in the marriage.

Their marital dramas had continued to cause Brad to relive his shame and reinforce that Carolyn was the innocent victim—the positions that both of them had inhabited during their childhoods. In the type of script that you read at the beginning of this chapter, he felt unjustly criticized, as he had been by his mother. This compelled him to explode into a rage, hurt Carolyn again, and abandon her by leaving their home for hours at a time. Then she could relive the shame of feeling unworthy of love in her childhood, as well as her anger at being mistreated.

The mutual crazy-making feeling that was still entirely nonconscious for both Brad and Carolyn was the enormity of their sorrow about the ongoing losses inherent in the deficiencies of the parenting they had received. The loss that they were consciously determined to avoid was that of their thirty-six-year marriage.

CHAPTER 6

Shame/Reunion Dramas

Charles and Kristine

K ristine was upset that Charles seemed to be reneging on his agreement to set a wedding date, but Charles was having serious reservations about getting married again. Kristine had been married once before; Charles had two previous marriages and a propensity to get involved in affairs. The two of them had been living together for about three years when they came to couples therapy.

Three or four sessions into the treatment, they looked at each other with somewhat sheepish grins, and Kristine asked Charles, "Should we tell her?" They then commenced to share their "dirty little secret" that they had become lovers when Charles was still married to his second wife and Kristine was barely divorced. They proceeded to reveal their repeated struggles in deciding who and when to tell, as well as their concerns about how the beginnings of their relationship were influencing their difficulties in moving toward marriage.

Their relationship had begun as a friendship which lasted for a couple of years before transitioning into sexual intimacy. They were both quite aware of the shame they felt about succumbing to an affair but expressed no regrets about ending up with each other. It was clear that both had had to endure some personal hell in order to "earn" the reward of being together. They had been lovers for four years, interrupted by a couple of years in which Charles felt compelled to go back to his second wife to see if he could make that marriage survive, while Kristine felt abandoned and alone.

Reciprocal Roles of Charles and Kristine

Kristine is the middle of five children in her family of origin. She was two years old when her mother gave birth to twins, and Kristine recalls feeling that she had to take care of herself from that time on. Independence was a strong value in her family, and she recounted stories in therapy of remembering her father's encouragement to always "pay her own way."

Charles described his mother as self-absorbed and needy of his attention. She had survived significant childhood trauma and loss herself, leading to relationships in which she dictated to others precisely how they must care for her. Charles' father was an unavailable alcoholic, and his one sister is significantly younger. So Charles was the chosen one to take care of his mother's needs.

These childhood experiences had led Charles and Kristine to adopt roles within their families of origin that created the matching relationship template shown in Figure 6.1.

Shame/reunion Dramas

Feeling shame is a universal and unavoidable experience for all human beings, and it is a highly significant component of the dramas in all marriages. Shame is the emotion that automatically accompanies experiences of knowing that we are capable of being bad.[1] It is that terrible pit in your stomach that you feel when a person who means a lot to you looks at you with disgust or horror because you have done something they hate or fear. It makes us shrink from the other's gaze to avoid feeling hated. Before we humans are capable of processing feelings cognitively, all feelings are

Figure 6.1. Matching relationship template of Charles and Kristine

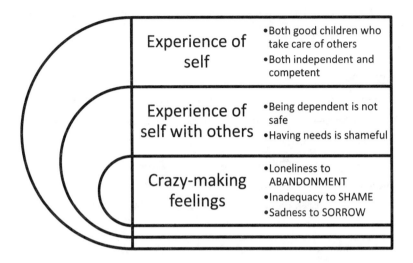

Experience of self	• Both good children who take care of others • Both independent and competent
Experience of self with others	• Being dependent is not safe • Having needs is shameful
Crazy-making feelings	• Loneliness to ABANDONMENT • Inadequacy to SHAME • Sadness to SORROW

experienced viscerally, so shame is an overwhelming whole-body experience that makes us feel pained in all ways when we are very young.

As we get older, our brains develop the ability to process emotions cognitively. Guilt is the feeling that accompanies being able to think about what our behavior *should* be. It comes along with developing a sense of morality and learning to follow the rules. People are capable of feeling guilty without feeling ashamed. Guilt is not so integrally entwined with one's sense of self. Being able to feel guilt helps us think, "I did a bad thing; I'd better not do that again." Feeling ashamed creates a much worse experience: "I *am* a bad thing; I guess no one is going to love me." So shame is about the "bad self" feeling shunned, banished, and disconnected from important others.[2]

Neuroscientists have discovered that our first experiences with shame occur in the first half of the second year of life.[3] At about fourteen months of age, toddlers begin to be mobile enough to explore and experiment with parts of life that were previously unavailable. In the process of taking this developmentally normal risk, they increase the likelihood that they will have their first experiences with their parents expressing disapproval of what they are doing, even if only to keep them safe from harm. The potentially crazy-making feeling that accompanies this disapproval is shame.[4]

Because toddlers have almost no tolerance for this new disrupting experience, they will often quickly seek repair by looking for some type of reconnection with their parents—a *reunion* of sorts to stop the unbearable feeling of being shunned. They need to experience that there is a way to get smiled at again—to get back into their parents' good graces. If the reunion occurs quickly enough to keep a child from becoming too dysregulated, and if there are not too many shaming words and looks coming from the parent, the reunion repairs the shame and prevents it from becoming a crazy-making feeling.[5]

I happened to have the opportunity to observe the origin of this cycle of shame and reunion when my grandson was exactly fourteen months old. Our family was enjoying dinner together at a pizza and burger restaurant where the seating is primarily wooden booths. Our grandson was standing on the seat between his parents on one side of the booth, and his mother had her arm around his waist. As dinner progressed, he became typically squirmy as toddlers do, and he kept leaning over his mother's pizza to grab his favorite part, the black olives. At a particular moment, our daughter-in-law seemed to become concerned that her little son might fall; she slightly tightened her grip around his waist and said quietly but firmly, "Stop it." He immediately stopped moving, and his eyes lowered as he focused on his own two hands—a manifestation of experiencing shame. His mother made him tolerate this state for only about one minute before she said "OK" in a playful, lilting voice and invited him to have some more pizza, thus completing the cycle with a repairing reunion of reconnection that the fourteen-month-old boy could experience as manageable.

In contrast, parents who too frequently resort to humiliation and ridicule in order to control their children's behavior or who get too personally wounded themselves when their children displease them will likely overwhelm the brains of their children with unhelpful shame. Subsequently, if these children are forced to tolerate an unbearable amount of time before the shame is repaired with a reunion or if—even worse— they are left to deal with the shame completely alone, their nonconscious storage bins will likely contain much unmetabolized shame.

As introduced in chapter 2, everyone's relationship template includes information about how this cycle of shaming and reunions contributes to our experiences of self with others. The responses of our primary caretakers to our bad selves during early childhood set up in our brains the particular cycle that must be repeated in marital dramas. As with other parts of the matching relationship template, the matching shame and reunion experiences of intimate partners are a highly compelling element in their attraction to each other. Unfortunately, this means that they are destined to wound each other in ways that seem the same as their parents did in order to get unmetabolized shame into present experience,[6] while at the same time connecting in ways dictated by the childhood reunions.

Let's return to our story of Charles and Kristine to clarify how shame/reunion dramas look in a marriage. You read above that both of their relationship templates had included dictates to be caretaking, independent children. Their experiences in childhood had taught them to literally feel ashamed for having normal human needs, because their parents' responses to their needs were anywhere from getting overwhelmed to accusing their children of being "selfish." Kristine and Charles had both suffered long periods of shame, guilt, and aloneness in their families of origin in order to be forgiven for having needs and thereby work their way back into reunions. This was the script they were repeating in their present relationship—express needs through having an affair with each other, feel ashamed, suffer through separation from each other, get back together, feel ashamed about having an affair, suffer through indecision about getting married, and on and on.

45

An important strategy that both Kristine and Charles had developed in childhood to atone for having needs was to compulsively put others' needs before their own. For Charles, this meant that he had to put the needs of both of his previous wives and of their children—even the ones who were not his own—before his needs. For Kristine, this meant she felt compelled to wait for Charles to decide that he was ready to marry again.

Kristine: "I thought that you said you would be willing to set a date in May."

Charles: "No, we can't do it then. That's when Amy [*his daughter*] wants to get married."

Kristine: [*with disappointment in her voice*] "OK, so when then?"

Charles: "Well, then I have my trip to Montana. Then, it will be summer vacation, and I promised to do some things with Diane's [*ex-wife*] kids."

Kristine: [*beginning to cry*] "But you promised *me* that we would talk about getting married this spring. We've lived together long enough; I don't want to keep going this way."

Charles: "This is when I start to get really nervous about getting married again. I've always had to do what everybody else wanted me to do or feel guilty if I don't. So it's just easier to be by myself."

The bind was the same for both Charles and Kristine—I can either be alone or feel ashamed. They didn't know that they could be in a marriage and not feel shamed by each other.

Even after they were eventually able to agree on a wedding date, the drama of shame followed by connecting through suffering continued. Kristine was worn out by her job. She had worked for the same insurance company for many years, but they had begun putting a lot of pressure on their employees to solicit more and more customers. She developed problems with her eyes, which she attributed both to the pressure she was under and to the many hours she spent at the computer every day. Charles had been encouraging her to quit her job for a long time, but Kristine couldn't get comfortable with the idea of letting him financially support her.

Charles: "Did you see the doctor again about your eyes?"

Kristine: "Yes. He still says that he thinks it's stress related."

Charles: "We've talked about this before. Why don't you just quit your job?"

Kristine: "I'm still trying to see if I can get a medical release to go part time or get on medical disability or something."

Charles: "But you know that I can financially support both of us, and you're under so much stress that you're unhappy most of the time."

Kristine: "I can't stand the idea of not having enough of my own money. I know that you've said you wouldn't mind if I depend on you for money, but I just can't get comfortable with it. I know that you will resent me for it someday."

Charles: "No, I won't. I'd rather pay for both of us than to have you be miserable all the time. That's all you talk about, and that's really no fun for me."

Kristine: "Charles, I just can't do it yet, OK?" [*The conversation ends with her crying.*]

After many attempts to get her company to let her work part time or give her some type of medical disability, she finally gave notice that she was resigning. Kristine was greatly relieved and grateful to Charles for helping her get away from that particular suffering, but she continued to express fears that Charles was harboring resentment because she was now partially dependent on his money. Her reliving of the shame/reunion drama had become: "Being dependent is shameful, and I will suffer by losing the affection of my partner."

The other types of marital dramas—dramas of opposites, competition dramas, and victims and villains dramas—are often variations of the shame/reunion drama as well. All of these contain the element of conflicts about the "bad self." Which one of us is really the bad one? Which one of us is worse? Which one deserves to be shunned and banished, and which one is perfectly innocent and has no "badness"? How our parents help us recover (or not) from the exposure of our naturally human inadequacies determines the particular shame/reunion drama that will be relived in every marriage.

Conclusion

The dramas of marriage are nature's way of providing us with the perfect opportunities to metabolize old, troublemaking emotions. You now know how our brains choose precisely the right partner for us with a relationship template that matches our own in order to experience scripted interactions that draw out the emotions waiting to be metabolized. These interactions develop into one or more of four types of dramas: 1) dramas of opposites; 2) competition dramas; 3) victims and villains dramas; and 4) shame/reunion dramas. The dramas are always perfectly constructed to help both partners relive in the present the same and/or complementary emotions from their childhoods.

This whole neuropsychologically generated process is immensely frustrating to intelligent, well-meaning adults who find themselves repeatedly feeling and acting like children in exactly the same ways over and over again. They try again and again to find ways to stop driving each other crazy, but their own brains compel them to keep recycling the same upsetting feelings into their current lives. Again, you now know that intimate partners have no choice about experiencing this pattern. What we *can* choose is learning to stop the inevitably destructive path of the dramas by harnessing their constructive power. Read on!

PART II

Changing for Good

CHAPTER 7

Turning Recycling Dramas into Repairing Dramas

U p to this point, you have been reading about the dramas of marriage that are designed by our brains for reliving in the present old, unmetabolized emotions from childhood. These recycling dramas end the same way every time, with the same unmetabolized emotions felt by both partners and with those emotions consciously assigned to the present behavior of the partners instead of to the past. These dramas literally recycle the old emotions from childhood back into the nonconscious storage bins of both partners to wait for another chance to be metabolized. This pattern of recycling dramas creates frustration and pain in the lives of marital partners, leading to distance instead of intimacy and often threatening the life of the marriage.[1]

The remainder of this book is devoted to helping you and your partner learn how to stop driving each other crazy by turning your recycling dramas into repairing dramas. You will discover how to transform these recycling dramas into the path of healing and growth that finishes the metabolizing of those old crazy-making feelings. Transforming recycling dramas with repetitive endings into repairing dramas with new endings is the great hope and promise of marriage.[2] Intimate relationships in which this transformation does *not* occur will eventually deteriorate— sometimes into divorce, sometimes into constant fighting, sometimes into boredom, and sometimes into a form of permanent distance that looks like tolerance. Couples who *do* accomplish this transformation will experience the immense joy of healing each other for good and having the most fulfilling life together that they could have imagined.

Let's begin our journey toward learning about this transformation by looking more closely at the exact nature of recycling and repairing dramas. Then you will be introduced to the steps you and your partner will need to master together in order to achieve the healing and growth that your brains chose each other to do.

Recycling Dramas

All of the scripted interactions you read in Part I signaled the beginning of recycling dramas. Both partners simultaneously relive emotions from their pasts and then blame each other for what they are feeling in the present. Maintaining the blaming stance in the present leads to repeatedly experiencing the same unsatisfactory endings to their dramas and literally recycling their old unmetabolized emotions back into their nonconscious storage bins to be relived again another day.

Recycling dramas are a response to the brain's wish to magically change the past by redoing it in the present.[3] The matching storage bins of intimate partners nonconsciously conspire to convince them that they are creating each other's misery in the present. This pattern supports a mutual wish to literally change history by influencing each other to behave differently in the present. This natural process is completely illogical but universally applied by all humans. Since unmetabolized emotions from the past are attached to danger, we are all fearful about experiencing them consciously. In recycling dramas, intimate partners nonconsciously "agree" to help each other avoid the permanent wounding of those crazy-making feelings from the past and pretend that they can undo the past by changing each other in the present.[4]

Recycling dramas are an attempt to metabolize the crazy-making feelings from the past without the pain associated with knowing that they originated in childhood and therefore cannot be changed. Assigning emotions to the present makes them feel "fixable" but instead truncates the whole process of metabolizing. As long as intimate partners assign the emotions they are feeling in recycling dramas only to their partners, they cannot continue the process that their brains are trying to start that would lead to repairing dramas.

Figure 7.1. Recycling dramas

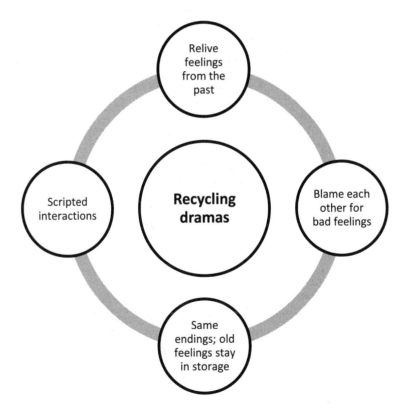

In chapter 1, you read the scripted interaction of Bill and Sally. Theirs was a competition drama that left both of them feeling lonely and abandoned. Here's what their recycling drama looked like:

Figure 7.2. Bill and Sally's recycling competition drama

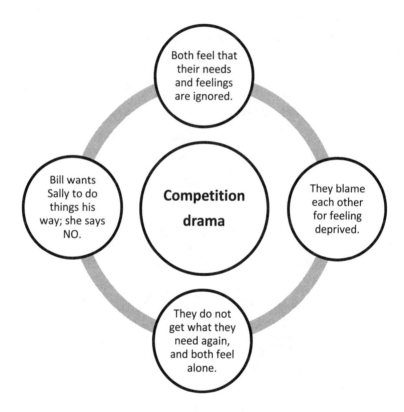

In my own marriage, ours was a recycling drama about shame and reunion. We found ourselves inadvertently and innocently recreating the feeling of shame that we had experienced as children when disappointing our parents. Then our reunions had to include some form of internal vow to never disappoint each other again.

Figure 7.3. Recycling shame/reunion drama in my marriage

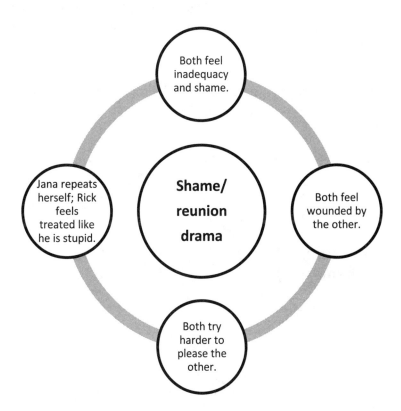

Repairing Dramas

Repairing dramas begin the same as recycling dramas, with the same scripted interactions dictated by the nonconscious storage bins that cause the reliving of the crazy-making feelings from childhood. Here the two types of dramas markedly diverge. Repairing dramas require the courage to realize that the pain both partners are *mutually* creating in the present originated long before they knew each other. Repairing dramas require an eagerness to talk about the old crazy-making feelings and the experiences in childhood that created those feelings. Intimate partners who want to heal each other through repairing dramas must empathize with each other's pain rather than blaming each other. They must understand and validate each other's past crazy-making feelings in order to take them out of storage and genuinely free themselves from the influence of the past for good.

Repairing dramas are nature's route for completing the metabolizing of the crazy-making feelings that have been part of both partners' relationship templates throughout their lives. Taking advantage of this

Figure 7.4. Repairing dramas

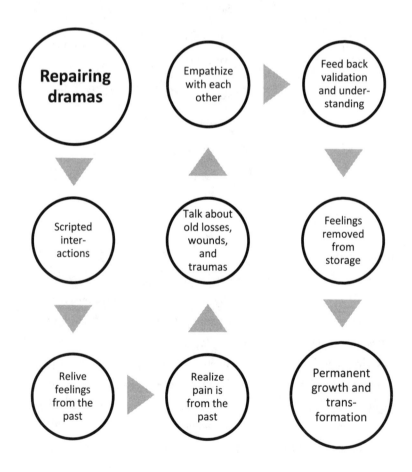

opportunity is not easy, to say the least. The great challenge in this process is that both partners will be reexperiencing their own unmetabolized emotions simultaneously. Managing the experience of both intimate partners reliving significant pain from childhood, *while maintaining their ability to be empathic instead of blaming*, is the key to staying on the repairing path—the key to being each other's healers rather than another form of each other's tormenters.

Here's how Bill and Sally turned their recycling competition drama into a repairing drama. They begin with the same scripted interaction:

Bill: "Let's go up to the condo this weekend."

Sally: "I don't want to go up to the condo this weekend."

Bill: "Why not? The skiing is supposed to be great."

Sally: "We just went last weekend, I have things I need to do at home, and I don't like skiing with you."

Bill: "Why don't you like skiing with me?"

Sally: "You have to go down all of the hardest runs, and it's no fun for me. I just ski for fun, not to see how many of the hardest runs I can do!"

Bill: "But I really want you to ski with me."

Sally: "No! Just go without me."

[*Both Bill and Sally fall silent while they try to think about their own emotions.*]

Bill: "We're doing this again—setting it up so we both have to be alone."

Sally: "Well, I don't want to have to ski the same runs with you."

Bill: "I'm trying to think about why I have such a hard time letting you ski where you want to, instead of on my runs." [*another pause*] "I guess I just want you to see what a good skier I am. When you're not there, it reminds me of how bad I felt when

	my parents never wanted to come to any of my sports. I was pretty good, and they never saw any of it." [*He looks down, and his pain is obvious.*]
Sally:	"My parents were always off doing their *own* sports instead of spending time with us kids." [*She looks down and takes a moment to come to a realization.*] "Huh. I guess I've always felt like you leave me like they did to go do your sport—that skiing every weekend is more important to you than I am."
Bill:	"I guess I've wanted both—to ski and to be with you. But now that I know what this is really all about, I think that it will be easier for me to have you come up with me and not feel bad when you don't ski with me. Then maybe we can both enjoy ourselves more. What do you think?"
Sally:	"We'll see, but next weekend would be better for me."
Bill:	"That's OK."

The scripted interactions in Sally and Bill's recycling dramas were created from the same self-protective and "selfish" roles that they had learned in their original families. In this repairing drama, they begin by reliving the same loneliness they felt as children. As Bill develops the courage to label their loneliness, he also begins to wonder why it is so important to him to coerce Sally into doing things his way. The more they talk without blaming, they begin to recall the abandonment of childhood that is being repeated between them. Placing the emotion of abandonment where it belongs in the past allows Sally and Bill to begin working on negotiating a ski trip that might work for both of them and not recycle loneliness and abandonment.

This type of repairing drama would need to be repeated many times in their marriage to fully metabolize their old crazy-making feelings.

Figure 7.5. Bill and Sally's repairing drama

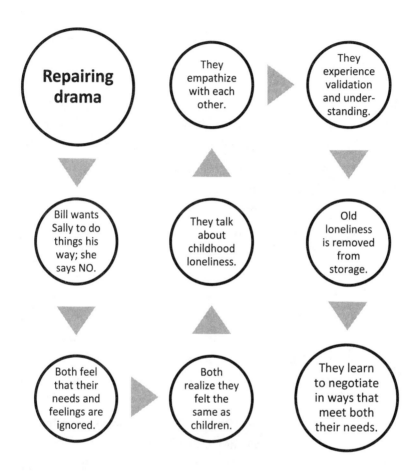

Here's how my husband and I turned the recycling shame/reunion drama you read above into a repairing drama:

Jana: "Could you have dinner ready for us about 7:30 this evening?"

Rick: "I think I can do that. I have a meeting that should be over about 6:00, so that'll work."

Jana: "So, you can have it ready at 7:30?"

Rick: "I heard you the first time. I'm not stupid, you know!"

Jana: *[feeling somewhat horrified, hurt, and mistakenly characterized]*
    "I would never think that you're stupid!"

[Both of us are feeling like bad children at this point. The shame is palpable, so a few moments of silence is necessary to regain our abilities to think like adults.]

Jana: "They made you feel really stupid, didn't they?" *[I already knew many of his stories about how he had been mistreated by his parents and his teachers during elementary school because they had no understanding of his learning disabilities.]*

Rick: "All the time." *[tears rimming his eyelids]*

Jana: "I'm so sorry that they didn't know any better how to help you. It's horrible for a kid to start his first contact with the world feeling so inadequate."

Rick: "It was pretty awful."

Jana: "I'll try really hard not to repeat myself, but my need to do that doesn't have anything to do with you. In my family, no one was listening to me, so I don't expect anyone to take in what I'm saying unless I repeat it."

[At this point, we are both fairly choked up and holding hands across the table.]

Rick: "It's OK. You ought to be able to say things as many times as you want without me reacting like that."

Jana: "Thanks. It's actually hard for me to let myself notice that you really do pay very close attention to me. I wish my family could have done that, and I'm probably trying to avoid the pain of knowing that they couldn't."

Figure 7.6. Repairing drama in my marriage

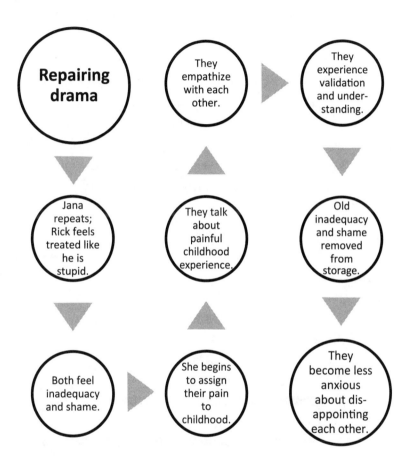

Preparing for Repairing Dramas

The examples of repairing dramas above clearly show that making the transition from recycling dramas to repairing dramas is challenging indeed. Being ready to move toward repairing dramas depends on the timing of each partner's willingness and readiness to courageously face the pain of the past. The magic of their psychological matching is that both partners are in the perfect position to create the experience of reliving their pasts, as well as the experience of perfect empathy for each other, but the timing has to be right for both partners to tolerate the unearthing of their losses, wounds, and traumas from childhood.

Timing might be determined by where each partner is in her or his psychological development. It might have something to do with whether or not this is the first marriage for both partners or one of a long series of intimate relationships. It might be about one or both partners reaching a chronological age or a number of years being together that has some concrete significance from their childhood histories. Or it might be driven by the threat of losing the marriage.

Figure 7.7. **Steps to transformation**

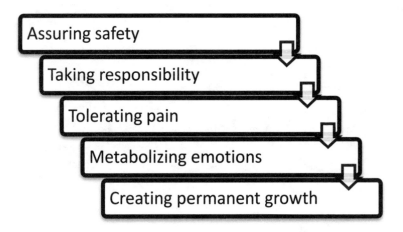

Getting ready for repairing dramas requires preparation. A couple must undertake these tasks together to prepare for the promised transformation of themselves and their relationship. Without performing all of these steps, the nonconscious part of their brains will not allow them to relinquish recycling dramas for repairing dramas.

TURNING RECYCLING DRAMAS INTO REPAIRING DRAMAS

The remainder of this book will describe in detail how you and your partner can accomplish these steps to transformation. You will observe the unfolding of several repairing dramas as you become immersed in others' paths to permanent healing and growth and thereby learn how to create your own. As you read the repairing dramas in the chapters that follow, you will clearly see how difficult it can be to turn recycling dramas into repairing dramas. The process takes substantial commitment and perseverance, as it is usually long and painful. The repetition of many repairing dramas is necessary in order to metabolize the crazy-making feelings that have been driving a recycling drama.

But the only alternative to accepting the challenge of repairing dramas is to live permanently in the distancing world of recycling dramas. The consequences of rejecting repairing dramas can be constant conflict, isolation, boredom, leading "parallel lives," or even divorce. The rewards of embracing them are almost boundless. You will read about the specific rewards our couples reaped in the final chapter.

CHAPTER 8

Assuring Safety

Opening ourselves up to true intimacy is very risky, so it makes a lot of sense that safety is paramount.[1] Our brains simply will not allow us to even know about the most vulnerable parts of ourselves—much less share them with another person—unless we are certain that we will be treated with care, compassion, and genuine understanding. We also need to know that revealing the worst within us will not lead to being left, so the safety of commitment to the relationship by both partners is a necessity.

Here I am speaking of safety in all senses of the word—physical, mental, emotional, sexual, and spiritual. If a couple cannot be physically safe with each other, that aspect of safety must be addressed first. Feeling physically threatened by one's partner precludes any kind of transformation together. In the mental and emotional realms, a safe couple can treat each other with mutual respect, whereas an unsafe couple is compelled to employ a judgmental and/or exploitive stance toward each other. Unsafe couples often use threats of divorce or other types of retaliation to get what they want. A safe couple is never deceptive or manipulative with each other; keeping their relationship safe is always more important to them than any individual triumph.

As stated in the introduction, the unmetabolized emotions that are sent to our nonconscious storage bins are attached to danger. So, naturally, these feelings themselves have a "not safe" tag on them. Partners who do not feel safe with each other cannot become conscious together of the emotions that are still needing to be metabolized, because their brains will be continuing to protect them from danger. The nonconscious storage bin will not open itself to the vulnerability of being experienced and examined until it is sure that abandonment, retraumatizing, and reshaming will not occur.

Rather than a final goal, I see safety as merely the beginning point of the process of taking advantage of the opportunity that our brains create for us when we choose a mate. The couples I have treated who were never able to establish adequate safety in their relationships ended up losing their marriages, because they could not make the transition from recycling to repairing dramas. Setting the stage for this transition requires accomplishing the following four tasks:

Figure 8.1. Safety requirements for repairing dramas

Maintaining Desire and Commitment

In order to heal and transform each other, a couple must truly *want* to be together.[2] My experience has been that couples cannot improve a relationship that one or both of them doesn't desire anymore. The causes for no desire are varied. Perhaps lack of safety in the relationship has gone on too long. Perhaps one partner has met someone new who represents an opportunity to escape the pressures of intimacy. Perhaps the partners have grown apart. Perhaps one or both partners never developed the ability to experience desire internally because they had to disown their dependency needs. Whatever the conscious reason, if one or both partners continually express a genuine desire to leave the relationship, transformation cannot proceed.

The nonconscious storage bin will not open itself to exploration if there is a threat of being left. Couples who resort to threatening separation or divorce when they are feeling helpless are seriously compromising their ability to ever feel safe enough with each other to create repairing dramas. The threats themselves are part of a recycling drama that must be interrupted as soon as possible in order to assure safety in the relationship. Repeatedly threatening to leave an adult relationship is perceived the same by the nonconscious storage bin as a parent saying to a child, "If you don't straighten up, I'll put you up for adoption!"

For example, in the marriage of Brad and Carolyn that you read about in chapter 5, their recycling dramas often ended with him leaving their house for long periods of time without letting Carolyn know when he would return home. Sometimes their scripted interactions included threats of divorce from either one of them, and of course, their marriage had been under actual threat of divorce when Brad was having his affair. In order to feel safe enough to engage in repairing dramas that would locate their fears of abandonment solely in their childhoods, they had to stop their leaving behaviors in their marriage.

The recycling dramas in the relationship between Kristine and

Charles that you read about in chapter 6 could not move toward repairing dramas until they set a wedding date. The safety of long-term commitment is necessary for the nonconscious storage bins to open to conscious experience and exploration. I get vehement push-back on this point often, but I am absolutely certain that repairing dramas will not occur unless the nonconscious in both partners' brains can feel that they are in a permanent commitment.[3] This usually requires marriage or some legal arrangement that our brains perceive as equivalent. All parts of your brain must feel like you are in a family again.

You will recall the earlier introduction in chapter 2 of the concept of the ecstasy feeling that occurs between mothers and infants. While maintaining sexual desire for each other is a necessary motivator for repairing dramas, couples whose experience of desire is *only* in the realm of sexual ecstasy are stuck in an early stage of development that will make it extremely difficult to move toward transformation. They are attempting to create an experience with each other that is available only to infants and their mothers—not to adult intimate partners. So all forms of desire must be at a more advanced developmental level than the fantasies of perfection that accompany the romantic phase of a relationship in order for the partners to be able to tolerate the exploration of their nonconscious storage bins.

A particular problem with desire arises in people whose early childhood experiences taught them that feeling anxious is the same as feeling excited. They learn to be stimulated and excited (a positive experience) by anxiety (a negative experience). In other words, they learn to be attracted to people who make them feel anxious. For example, the brain of a person who continues to yearn for another who is chronically unavailable—as in "playing hard to get"—has fused anxiety and excitement in a way that automatically connects emotional danger and desire. Worse yet are those people who are attracted to irresponsible, risk-taking behavior. Couples who confuse anxiety and excitement must learn that danger isn't exciting—that it isn't normal for your partner to make you feel bad—in order to establish true safety in their connection.

Often it happens that one or both partners are ambivalent in their desire; they aren't sure they want to stay. This ambivalence can be a manifestation of the closeness/distance rules that are part of the relationship template. Ambivalence can also be about one or both partners imagining that their lives would be better with a different partner. They want to think that they simply chose the wrong partner and that all of their problems will magically disappear if they are with someone else.

Until both partners are ready to know that their own issues will simply be repeated in all of their intimate relationships, they will be tempted to escape instead of taking the journey to deeper levels of intimacy and healing. A couple is not safe to experience repairing dramas until both of them are certain that they want to continue the relationship and that they are committed to staying together through the painful moments that they will share.

Treating Each Other with Respect

The work of an esteemed researcher in the area of marital relationships, John Gottman, focuses on the behaviors that he has found most often lead to divorce.[4] He states that couples who approach each other with contempt and disdain are at risk of losing their marriages. They have lost their ability to treat each other with respect.

This aspect of safety seems rather obvious really, but many people do not learn how to treat others in their families with respect. In fact, they often seem to learn the opposite—that you can be the meanest to the people you live with! Yelling and screaming at each other triggers a fight, flight, or freeze response and stirs up the brain to the point that one can focus only on trying to get unscrambled and escape danger. Assuring safety requires treating each other's feelings with care. That means not using inflammatory and derogatory language to speak to each other. It also means not attaching discounting and demeaning labels to each other's character.

When couples are enacting their recycling dramas, they have experiences with each other in reliving their old crazy-making feelings that can lead to a distorted picture of who their partner really is. Because their nonconscious storage bins have "trained" each other to relive unmetabolized emotions from the past, they begin to conclude things about each other's character that aren't true. They begin to call each other "selfish," "childish," "moody," "abusive," and many more labels that can get pretty nasty. Couples who can't drop this labeling habit will not be able to move toward repairing dramas. Obviously, if they are hateful toward each other, they cannot be safe.

Refusing the Victim or Villain Role

Couples with one or both partners who are determined to view themselves as the victim cannot begin the transformation process until both relinquish this position. Although each partner's behavioral patterns that have contributed to repetitive problems may be quite different, they must both be able to see their part and own responsibility for having *equally* contributed to their recycling dramas in order to participate in a transformation process. Neither feeling like a victim *nor being accused of being a villain* is a safe position from which to open up to the examination of oneself within a marriage.

It seems unfortunate that *feeling like* a victim is an inevitable part of many recycling dramas. As you read about in chapter 4, Karen and Bob had both been genuine victims of horrible childhood abuse and abandonment. Because their matching crazy-making feelings from childhood had to be relived, they continually felt victimized by each other and continually argued about which one was the real perpetrator who had started the whole mess. It was extremely difficult for both of them to relinquish the role of victim and stop characterizing the other one as the villain in order to establish safety in their relationship.

It is usually quite challenging to separate the reliving of our childhood crazy-making feelings from the reality we might be living in our marriages. In the marriages of both Katherine and Cynthia that you read about earlier, their experiences of having to do "everything" was a reliving of the roles from their childhoods in which they were truly overburdened by their parents' inabilities to accept adult responsibilities. Their need to relive doing everything and suffering at the hands of their "irresponsible" husbands was the recycling of true victimizing from childhood, although it was quite difficult to keep from assigning the blame to their husbands. John and Matthew were in the unsafe position of being characterized as the villain, as reliving their unmetabolized emotions dictated that they assume the role of letting their wives down.

Refusing to continue accepting either the victim or the villain role that your recycling dramas may have assigned to you is an essential element in moving on to repairing dramas. Both partners must be operating from a position of equal power, equal vulnerability, and equal responsibility for their own words and behaviors in order to assure safety.

Taking Responsibility
This aspect of assuring safety is so integral to creating repairing dramas that I have dedicated the entire next chapter to understanding it.

CHAPTER 9

Taking Responsibility

In order for both partners to trust each other enough to be open and vulnerable, they must both be able to take responsibility for their own thoughts, emotions, and behaviors. People who have to blame others for what they think, feel, and do are not developmentally ready to use their intimate relationships for healing. It is a common tendency to believe that both our emotions and our behaviors are natural reactions to another's behavior. In other words, *you* are *making me* feel or act this way. This experience is a derivative of being someone's child. Our partners might seem to be creating a certain reaction, but each partner's participation in the marital dramas generates his or her own emotions and behaviors.

Both partners must also be able to observe their own behavior honestly and with genuine curiosity and interest, instead of always responding defensively. They must be able to give feedback to each other in a safe and caring manner that neither blames nor shames their partner. They must exercise restraint with expressions of emotions, instead of instantly gratifying a need to expel them onto their partner. The individual psychologies of the partners have matured enough to advance toward repairing dramas when they stop focusing on changing their partner and become curious about how their *own* behavior is contributing to their recycling dramas.[1]

Adults don't blame others for their plights. They don't blame others for their emotions and behaviors or make others responsible for their needs. Becoming an adult means relinquishing the wish to have another chance at childhood. It means that we are ready to deal with accepting that the traumas and wounds of childhood represent permanent losses that must be consciously felt and metabolized.

In order to assure safety in your intimate relationship by taking responsibility, you must be able to consistently perform the following tasks:

Figure 9.1. Taking responsibility

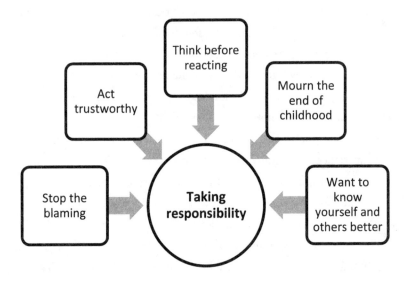

Stopping the Blaming

It seems so logical to assume that other people's behaviors create our reactions. In fact, you have already read that an integral piece of the process of the development of an infant is the mutual "dance" that is going on between a child and a caretaker in which they are both involved in a reciprocal influencing of each other's emotions and behaviors. Research into the attachment patterns of human beings has taught us this fact.[2]

By the time we get to adulthood, our relationship templates that form out of these childhood attachment patterns will have much more influence over how we react to our partners than what is happening in the present. As the nonconscious storage bins of intimate partners "teach" each other how to enact their recycling dramas, they will learn the behaviors that must be used to relive the old crazy-making feelings. So it is each person's nonconscious storage bin that dictates how he or she will feel and act—not the present event. As I stated earlier, the present event is like the starter of a car; the emotions in the nonconscious storage bins are the "engine" that keep the feelings going.

Blaming another for how you feel or behave is the same as playing the role of victim. It is essentially saying, "I have no control over myself. You are the one with the power to force me to feel and/or act this way." Couples cannot possibly engage in repairing dramas unless both of the partners take control of their own behavior and expressions of emotions.

Can people be unnecessarily irresponsible in their attempts to provoke an emotion in another? Absolutely, but no one can make someone else feel or do something if the person on the receiving end of a possible provocation maintains control. It is interesting to note that this belief that we cause others' internal experience is much less prevalent in the case of trying to make someone feel good. We seem much more willing to accept that we don't have the power to force positive feelings on another than negative feelings.

Stopping the blaming also means not blaming yourself. All of us are human, meaning that we have a nonconscious storage bin that compels us to feel and behave in ways that may seem consciously foreign. Finding fault with yourself or with others may be beneficial in certain parts of life's troubles where it is necessary to assign culpability. But not in our intimate relationships with our partners, particularly when we are trying to use those relationships to heal old wounds and traumas. Blaming leads to shaming, and the nonconscious part of our minds will not feel safe to be exposed if the unmetabolized emotions are being judged as good or bad. Assuring safety requires taking responsibility for our own emotions and behaviors without blaming ourselves or others.

Acting Trustworthy

Trustworthiness is about dependability and consistency. Trusting people means that you can count on them to tell the truth, to do what they tell you they will do, and to not keep secrets from you. You simply cannot feel safe with someone who can't be trusted. Any marriage in which the recycling dramas include chronic lying or secrets like affairs cannot move toward repairing dramas until these patterns are interrupted.

One of the most challenging aspects of repairing dramas is the requirement to be absolutely honest about our own feelings—honest to ourselves and honest to our partners. Many of us were taught in childhood that we must protect others from our bad feelings, so we might have been encouraged to deny how we are truly feeling. Repairing dramas require the courage to be truthful about our emotions, even if we are concerned that our own expressions might hurt our partners. It is highly probable that the hurt our partners might feel is in fact an essential ingredient in a repairing drama to metabolize old hurt feelings.

Acting trustworthy precludes "mind reading." Each partner must be able to trust that his or her self-expressions will be believed instead of questioned. Reacting to your partner from a position of "I know you better than you know yourself" is highly unsafe. Our brains get fooled into thinking that mind reading is an essential part of intimate connections, because mothers of infants are required to try to guess what their children are needing. Attuned mothers get good at knowing what their babies are experiencing, so the brain records a type of mind reading as part of the feelings associated with closeness. In living with your partner, you will certainly observe patterns of behavior, but assigning negative feelings, thoughts, and motivations to those behaviors is not safe, particularly if your partner denies having those feelings, thoughts, and motivations.

For example, in the recycling drama from my marriage that you read above, my husband's role compelled him to experience my thinking of him as stupid, in order to bring the old, crazy-making feelings associated with that experience from childhood into the present. In order for both of us to be safe enough to engage in a repairing drama, he had to believe me when I told him that I would never think of him as stupid.

Sometimes we can be so afraid to bring up difficult emotions with our partner that we resort to talking with a third party—our best friend, our parents, a coworker, or even a new lover. We keep secrets from our partner and develop intimacies that can be quite unsafe to the marital relationship. The professional literature calls this *triangulation*.[3] Many recycling dramas use triangulation as a means to deal with our fears and avoid responsibility for our own feelings. Again, it can require great courage to take the risk to be safely honest and direct with our partner. This type of trust is essential to creating repairing dramas.

Thinking before Reacting

In the presentation of the repairing dramas above, you read references to one or both partners taking time to think or "get their adult brains back." When our brains feel flooded with old unmetabolized emotions from childhood, we are reliving the dysregulated state that is dominated by the nonconscious storage bin. Crazy-making feelings are stored because our brains have correctly sensed that these feelings were too unmanageable to be aware of when they originally occurred. So when they come out of storage in a recycling drama, the same level of threat is attached, making it quite difficult to respond from an adult, rational level.

Being reactive—automatically responding without thinking—is counterproductive to transformation. It is a recycling behavior that requires conscious focus to interrupt. Adult brains should be able to stay regulated under threat of difficult emotions better than child brains can. But when old unmetabolized crazy-making feelings come out of storage, the child brain has been spontaneously engaged, and it experiences these emotions *precisely as dysregulating as they were when originally stored.* It takes commitment, restraint, and the ability to tolerate pain to contain ourselves long enough to access adult thinking.[4] It also takes believing that knowing ourselves and our partners more deeply through repairing dramas is the route to true happiness.

Mourning the End of Childhood

You have read about why our human psychologies want to believe that we can redo childhood with our intimate partners. Pretending that the traumas and losses of childhood can be made to magically disappear by "undoing" them in our marriages is a tactic universally applied by all adult brains.[5] Childhood is the only chance we get to be unconditionally loved and have someone else take total responsibility for our needs. Facing the permanent ending of that chance can be so daunting that the nonconscious storage bins must support the fantasy that childhood can somehow be recaptured.[6]

The concept of mourning the end of childhood may sound foreign to some. Don't we go from being children to adults without giving it much thought? Don't we look forward to growing up and being in control of our own lives? These ideas represent the conscious memories that most of us have about transitioning from childhood into adulthood. In fact, all developmental progressions in our lives cause the loss of the benefits of the prior stage of life. Since the transition from childhood into adulthood represents the most significant changes in our life circumstances, it also contains the most loss. Mourning the end of childhood is about being consciously aware that we will never have another chance to experience the benefits of childhood. If we didn't get to experience some of those benefits because of our parents' developmental deficiencies, grieving those losses will be particularly painful.

Couples must be ready to relinquish the wish to be someone's child again before they can be someone's partner. The wish to continue childhood precludes taking responsibility for our own needs. Grown-up intimacy requires that an individual has the ability to attend to his or her self-needs *and* the needs of the connection with the partner *simultaneously*. Nonconsciously desiring the continuation of childhood causes a person to stay unaware of these requirements and instead to try to get the partner to take care of him or her without regard for the needs of the adult relationship between them.[7]

Mourning the end of childhood motivates intimate partners to turn to each other for their adult dependency needs, instead of continuing the search for child dependency needs either from their partner or their parents (or worse still, an extramarital relationship). Accepting that the benefits of childhood are gone for good allows them to effectively and finally turn their recycling dramas into repairing dramas. Couples who are ready to consciously mourn with each other the permanent loss of the childhoods they wish they had experienced are ready for repairing dramas and the resulting freedom to finish growing up together.

Genuinely Wanting to Know Yourself and Your Partner Better
When Bill and Sally were working on a repairing drama, he wondered why he had such strong emotions about wanting Sally to ski the hard runs with him. Bill became curious about himself. Genuinely wanting to know yourself and your partner better means that you are more curious about each other's inner experiences than you are determined to change your partner's behavior.[8] The goal of the repairing drama is to make it safe for old emotions to get metabolized—not to determine whose behavior is wrong and therefore must change. Simply changing behavior without wanting to know about the emotions driving the behavior is another form

of recycling drama. Crazy-making feelings from childhood will find a way to get relived, even if new behaviors are employed.

As couples experience their recycling dramas, they can begin to see aspects of their partners revealed that seem to make no sense or are just plain irritating. A safe stance from which to transform into repairing dramas is to assume that all of our partners' behaviors and emotions are understandable when their origins are known.[9] This is what Sally and Bill discovered in their repairing drama. The strong emotions that were driving their old recycling drama were completely understandable as they learned to link them to past patterns with their parents. Containing and taking responsibility for each of their own emotions—being more curious about how they were both feeling in the moment—became more important to each of them than getting their own way and thereby recycling loneliness.

The most challenging moments to maintain curiosity are those times when you and your partner have very different memories of a past event. It can be extremely compelling to get into a recycling competition drama to establish whose memory is "right," but arguing about which one of you remembers the past correctly is futile and unsafe.[10] A repairing drama requires entering into a genuinely curious state of mind about the meanings of your differing memories in order to understand the unmetabolized emotions that are attempting to rise to consciousness. Everyone's memory is highly subjective, particularly during experiences in our intimate relationships. Being interested in the *emotions* represented in memories must be more important than establishing objective "truth" about what happened.

Couples who desire to safely know each other will focus on what is going on in their own heads, instead of focusing on analyzing their partner. They think, "I wonder what *I* am feeling" more than "I know what *you're* feeling." In spite of how well you think you know your partner, it is not safe to presume that you know more about how your partner is feeling than he or she does. You might be projecting your *own* feelings onto your partner. Genuinely wanting to know yourself and your partner better means letting each one of you be the expert in his or her own thoughts and feelings and taking responsibility for expressing them safely to each other.

CHAPTER 10

Tolerating Pain

O ur brains need all of the steps to transformation that you have read above to prepare them for tolerating conscious awareness of the old crazy-making feelings. As stated earlier, we cannot know about emotions that are correctly experienced as too dangerous. Being ready for metabolizing stored emotions is signaled by the ability to tolerate the emotional pain that will always accompany old feelings.[1]

The heartache that is triggered by becoming aware of old losses, wounds, and traumas is often deep, intense, and much more prolonged than we want to believe it can be. We want to assign our pain to the present, make it shorter, ignore it, or pretend that it is someone else's pain. The vast majority of harm in our closest relationships is caused by the inability to tolerate emotional pain. A person who cannot tolerate his or her own pain will be absolutely compelled to create distance from loved ones. Parents who cannot tolerate their own pain create feelings of rejection, shame, and fear in their children, because the parents cannot stay engaged when they are feeling their own intolerable emotions.

Tolerating is about staying with our emotional pain and owning it, even when we become very uncomfortable. When you and your partner are ready to begin the metabolizing process together, you will likely be astounded at how much pain remains in your nonconscious storage bins, and you must know that you can bear feeling it with each other.

In the examples of repairing dramas that you read in chapter 7, both couples had to tolerate feeling pain and then be able to think about what was going on between them in order to transform a recycling drama into a repairing drama. Bill had to tolerate the pain of having his wife tell him again that she did not want to ski with him, contain himself, and think about what was happening in order to discover that the vast majority of his pain was about the past with his parents. Being aware that coercing his wife into doing what he wanted would never erase the pain of what his parents couldn't do released him to enter into a repairing interaction about the old crazy-making feelings from the past that they were both experiencing in the present.

In the repairing drama from my marriage, I had to tolerate the pain of being accused of treating my husband as if he were stupid. Thinking before I reacted allowed me to empathize with the massive pain from his childhood, during which he was truly treated as stupid. For my husband to take in my empathy, he also had to tolerate conscious awareness of that old pain, instead of insisting that I was creating all of it in the present.

Metabolizing Emotions
Once a couple has assured safety in their relationship, taken responsibility for their own feelings and behaviors, and learned to tolerate emotional pain, they are ready for the next step to transformation. Metabolizing the old crazy-making feelings from both of their childhoods is what their brains chose each other to do, and it is the whole point of the marital dramas they have been creating together.[2] In the following five chapters, we will look in depth at the process of metabolizing the emotions that are most often being recycled in marital dramas (shown in Figure 2.2).

You may have noticed that I did not include anxiety in the list of unmetabolized emotions commonly relived in marriages. While some authors would categorize anxiety as an emotion, others think of it differently. I see anxiety as a precursor—a type of sentinel, if you will—that precedes an emotion. People feel anxious when their brains are saying to them, "Watch out! There might be an emotion coming that you don't want/can't stand to feel." The anticipation of an unknown or not previously experienced outcome can trigger anxiety.[3] Since our brains correctly perceive the emotions they have stored as too dangerous for conscious awareness, the threat of actually feeling them can make us anxious. Learning to manage the anxiety that usually precedes unexperienced emotions is a necessary ingredient to setting the stage for tolerating the emotional pain that comes with repairing dramas.

In the next five chapters, you will read many repairing dramas that the couples you've gotten to know in this book courageously constructed together in order to metabolize the crazy-making feelings in their matching relationship templates. You will also read about the preparation that each couple had to accomplish before they could attempt repairing dramas. Because real human experiences are not conveniently tidy, marital dramas are seldom about metabolizing only one emotion. For purposes of illustration, most of the repairing dramas shared in the next five chapters are primarily about one emotion, while some address more than one.

In the "Unmetabolized Emotions" chart in chapter 2, the emotions are listed in the order of difficulty for experiencing and metabolizing. The chapters that follow present the same order of emotions. This order is consistent with the developmental progression of human beings in their ability to deal with states of being, significance of losses, and depth of meaning. It is usually necessary for couples to construct repairing dramas about emotions at the younger end of the developmental scale before moving on to repairing dramas at the more complex and deeply wounding end of the spectrum. For example, a couple will probably need

85

to metabolize fear and anger before their nonconscious storage bins can feel safe enough to tackle shame or sorrow.

Before we look at the metabolizing of the emotions that couples most often are repeating in their marital dramas, I am going to introduce you to one more couple whose recycling dramas created a great deal of emotional pain for both of them in the present. I will illustrate through their story how all of the elements of the dramas of marriage that you have read about so far come together to create recycling dramas. Their story, along with the others to whom you have already been introduced, will be used to illustrate the metabolizing of all of the types of old crazy-making feelings in our nonconscious storage bins in chapters 11 through 15.

Richard and Carol

This couple was referred for marital treatment by Richard's individual therapist, who described him as one of the most depressed persons she had ever seen. He had been treated for depression since he was in college with various combinations of medications and other therapies. The marriage was quite fragile when they began treatment. They were talking about a separation, and as revealed later in the therapy, Richard had recently been involved in at least one affair and frequently fantasized about being with other women. He said that he simply was not attracted to his wife anymore, and he did not know if he wanted to stay in the marriage. Carol, on the other hand, was adamant about not getting a divorce.

Richard and Carol had met in college. Although he was studying to be a financial analyst, his real love was painting. Carol was also an artist, and this was a conscious part of the basis for their attraction to each other. Their relationship had always been somewhat tumultuous; both of them had strong personalities, and they had experienced many struggles along the way in charting the course of their relationship. The pattern of these struggles often took the form of Carol pursuing Richard to define where he stood with her, as he was often ambivalent.

Now in his thirties and about ten years into a marriage, Richard was still struggling with ambivalence about all of the important aspects of his life. He suffered continual angst about his career, vacillating between the corporate business world vs. being a full-time artist. He was not sure if he wanted to stay with Carol, and he certainly did not know if he wanted to start the family she clearly wanted. Although Carol had a job as an art teacher, she was quite dissatisfied with her place of employment. And she was still grieving the death of her mother from cancer approximately a year before the marital therapy started. These were two people in lots of pain.

Family Histories

Carol is the only child of her mother and her mother's second husband. Her mother's first husband had died in an industrial accident. That pair had a daughter—Carol's older half-sibling. Although Carol remembered being close to her father when she was very young, that had changed as she matured. They had difficulty understanding each other, because the important values in their lives were quite different. Her father had remarried a few months after the death of Carol's mother, and Carol felt that she was left with almost no connection with him and his new wife. All of the losses in her family had had a significant effect on Carol, some which she was aware of and some not.

Richard basically hated most of his family, and he put a sizable amount of effort into avoiding contact with them. Both of his parents were alcoholics, although his father was recovering when I saw Richard and Carol in treatment. His parents had been divorced since he was in college, and both of them had remarried. The extended family was ruled by a matriarch—Richard's maternal grandmother—whose husband owned and ran the family business of a chain of hardware stores in the Midwest. She acted as if she felt entitled to run everyone's life. Richard was the only one who had rebelled against the family rules and expectations; his two younger brothers were the "good kids." In recent years, Richard had held onto an improved relationship with his father, often visiting him in his vacation home and going fishing together, but he was still distant from everyone else in his family.

Reciprocal Roles in Richard and Carol's Recycling Dramas

Carol and Richard's scripted interactions created dramas of opposites, of victims and villains, and shame/reunion dramas. Both of them depended on her to provide the glue that held their relationship together, since she did not experience herself as ambivalent about much of anything. When Richard's affairs and attractions to other women were revealed during treatment, it was Carol who convinced him to keep working on the marriage, even as they lived through a marital separation for several months.

During their courtship, Carol had taken on the role of pursuer. At every step of their developing relationship, she had been the one to ask for a defining commitment from Richard. They both seemed to have some conscious wishes that getting married would resolve Richard's ambivalence, but of course that didn't happen. Even when his affair was over, he still found himself imagining that being with another woman or being away from his wife would somehow feel better. Getting married had not only failed to resolve his fears; it had made them worse. His fears about dependency, closeness, loss of self, and being controlled by significant others were greatly stimulated by becoming a husband.

Richard feared closeness because in his experience with his family of origin, closeness meant sameness and the entitlement to control another's behavior. He was terrified that being close to Carol would mean abandoning his individuality and his ability to say no to her. His childhood history with closeness had taught him not to trust it, so he created distance from Carol by continually imagining that she was inadequate as a wife. This recycling drama kept both of them in the position of experiencing their emotional pain as originating in their present circumstances, instead of in their childhoods.

The reciprocal roles that Carol and Richard played in the marriage kept them from being aware of how they had gotten harmed in their families of origin. Richard wanted to focus his ambivalence on everything except his family. He wanted to believe that his hatred of them for how they had interfered with his development of a separate self was unconflicted. Admitting ambivalence toward his family would mean admitting to himself that part of him still loved and needed them. That was too painful, so he consciously fueled the belief that he simply hated them and reserved his ambivalent feelings for Carol.

Figure 10.1. Matching relationship template of Richard and Carol

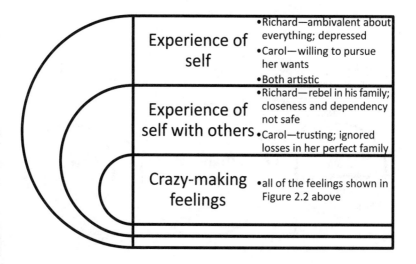

Richard's role of ambivalence in the marriage matched the need of Carol's nonconscious storage bin to relive her mother's ambivalent feelings toward her, although it was the opposite of her conscious representation of her mother as all-loving. Carol's mother had never

recovered from the loss of her first husband. As the child of the "substitute husband," Carol had not been embraced and loved the way her older half-sister had. Her continual struggles to keep Richard engaged in their relationship were a perfect script for reliving the manner in which she had related to her mother. Mothers are not supposed to be ambivalent toward their daughters, and the pain associated with Carol's awareness that her mother was conflicted about her attachment to Carol could be kept safely stored away by marrying Richard. She could focus on begging Richard to stay in the marriage, rather than being conscious of the emotions she had experienced when longing for her mother's love.

Figure 10.2. **Richard and Carol's recycling drama of opposites**

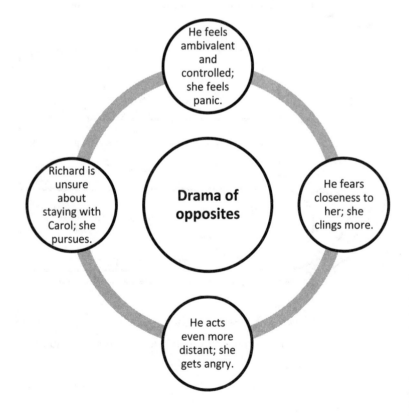

The dramas of opposites in this marriage were designed to keep both Richard and Carol unaware that the pain in their childhoods was equal. Richard was quite conscious of his negative feelings toward his family. He frequently reported dreams about his continuing rage and hatred toward them for their mistreatment of him. It sometimes made Carol uncomfortable for Richard to purposefully and directly reject his family of origin, although she agreed that their treatment of him in the past had been poor and that their current behavior could still be outrageously intrusive and controlling.

On the other hand, *both* Carol and Richard saw her family as almost perfect. There was a nonconscious agreement not to notice the ways in which they were unsupportive of her growth and development. A clinical way of stating it is they idealized her family of origin and devalued his. So none of their genuine crazy-making feelings about how they had been treated (and were still being treated) by their families could be given free expression.

Couples who enter the world of extramarital affairs are concretely and dramatically reliving the need to portray one of them as the victim and the other as the villain. Turning each partner into a half-baked caricature of the "good guy" and the "bad guy" performs the function of allowing each of them to experience only half of the crazy-making feelings that both of them stored in childhood. The particular dynamics within Carol and Richard's matching relationship template compelled them to relive this way of being together.

Richard was the "bad" child in his family of origin. He had been the rebel—the one who risked developing his own individuality instead of complying with the control of his parents and grandparents. Recycling the role of bad guy in the marriage kept him away from conscious awareness of the intolerable pain associated with knowing that he had been a genuine victim of his parents' inability to help him with his growth and development. He hadn't been a bad child; he had been a struggling child.

Carol had tried very hard in her childhood to be a good enough child to earn her mother's approval and affection. Recycling the role of victim

Figure 10.3. Richard and Carol's recycling victims and villains drama

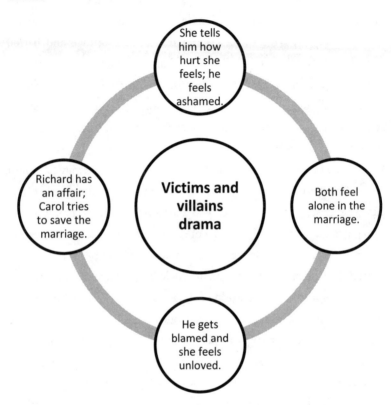

in her marriage kept her away from conscious awareness of the intolerable pain associated with knowing that her mother's unresolved grief about the loss of her first husband had prevented her from being able to love her second daughter as unconditionally as her first. Carol's working to be a better child wasn't going to change her mother's ability to love her, any more than being a victim in her marriage would change her childhood.

Both Carol and Richard were recycling their childhood shame through the dramas of affairs and a marital separation. He could relive the shame of being seen as a bad child through initiating an affair and pushing for a marital separation. At the same time, she was reliving the shame of

Figure 10.4. Richard and Carol's recycling shame/reunion drama

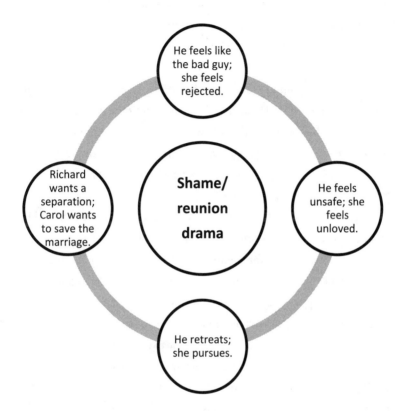

being rejected by her mother. Deep within both of their nonconscious storage bins was tremendous shame associated with a shared fear that they were simply unlovable people, because their childhood reunions had required denying their true selves. They had been compelled to do everything the others' way, and they were terribly afraid that it would simply be the same story in their marriage.

Preparing for Repairing Dramas

This marriage was highly unsafe and on the brink of total disintegration when Richard and Carol first came to treatment. They had to start their road to transformation at square one—maintaining desire and commitment. They were on opposite pages about their desire to keep the marriage, but they were both committed enough to keep working on the marriage in therapy during a six-month marital separation. They also agreed to express that commitment by eliminating all the secrets in their relationship and by accepting equal responsibility for the current state of disarray in their marriage. Richard admitted awareness that the relationships he had had with other women eventually felt the same as the one with Carol—he always felt stifled, controlled, and manipulated. So he was ready to stop thinking he could escape his emotions in the marriage by being with another woman.

In spite of their difficulties, they had always maintained their ability to be mostly respectful toward each other, which greatly contributed to a safe environment for talking together. However, both Carol and Richard had some work to do around conscious awareness of their own emotions. Because she was more emotionally reactive, their recycling dramas had led to a repetition of neither one of them knowing the true nature of their own internal messages. She expressed all of the emotions for both of them, effectively making it almost impossible to know whose feelings were whose. Genuinely wanting to know themselves helped both of them take clearer responsibility for recognizing and labeling their own emotions.

As is often the case, the task that was the hardest for them was mourning the end of childhood. They wanted to believe that their recycling dramas would magically end in fixing their childhood pain. Richard wished that having Carol tolerate a marital separation would erase the pain about his parents' inability to tolerate the assertion of his independence. And Carol wished that being patient while Richard decided to want her would erase the pain of her mother's rejection.

As we worked on making it safe for them to give up these understandable wishes, they gradually became more and more adept at tolerating the pain of knowing the exact nature of what was missing in their childhoods. Creating a safe space for exploring all of the emotions connected to their childhood losses and accepting that those emotions would never spontaneously evaporate through recycling dramas made Carol and Richard ready to begin the process of metabolizing the old, crazy-making feelings that had attracted them to each other in the first place.

CHAPTER 11

Metabolizing Emotions: Fear and Anger

F ear and anger are two powerful emotions that humans experience early in life,[1] because they are attached to the natural protective functions in our brains that perceive danger in the environment. Babies don't have any conscious thoughts about fear and anger. They express fear with what we see as a spontaneous startle response, and their anger is expressed through the cry of protest. All attuned parents know when their babies are showing one of these emotions.

The more primitive and overwhelming forms of these emotions— terror and rage—arise from the brain's automatic fight, flight, or freeze response to threat. Terror causes the flight or freeze responses, and rage generates the fight response. I want to emphasize that both of these emotions are self-protective in nature. They are about correctly perceiving a genuine threat to our well-being. The perceived threats that can evoke either or both of these crazy-making feelings are annihilation (death), abandonment, or the removal of resources needed for survival.[2]

These two important emotions are intertwined with each other and often hide behind each other. A person may be expressing anger when he or she is actually afraid. Another may be too fearful to express the actual rage she or he is feeling, because of the danger attached to the anger. You will also see in the repairing dramas that follow that marital partners often split these two emotions between them, with one person expressing anger and the other fear, even though both emotions are in both nonconscious storage bins. This is almost always the case in dramas of opposites.

Cynthia and Matthew

Cynthia: "We just got a notice from our mortgage company that we are behind on our payments. You told me that you would take over paying the mortgage."

Matthew: "Oh, no! I forgot to send it in."

Cynthia: [*with great dismay and disgust*] "I can't believe you forgot! You promised that you would take care of this! What if we lose the house?"

Matthew: "I'm sorry; I just forgot. What is wrong with me?"

Cynthia: "How could you be so irresponsible? Do I have to do EVERYTHING?"

Both Cynthia and Matthew are feeling threatened and unsafe in this scripted interaction, with Cynthia experiencing the anger and Matthew experiencing the fear (and shame).

This recycling drama provides the opportunity for both of them to feel these emotions in real time. So how are they going to turn this type of interaction into a repairing drama? Here's how they did it.

They started with reiterating their mutual desire to keep their marriage. In spite of beginning their search for resolution with the thought that their only choice was divorce, they didn't really want that. In many ways, they enjoyed their lives together, but they knew that they needed to change the way they were relating to each other—Cynthia being the "parent" and Matthew being the "child."

Figure 11.1. Cynthia and Matthew's recycling drama of opposites

For this couple, preparing for repairing dramas mostly meant that they needed to recognize their equal participation in the old dramas. Cynthia had to be willing to relinquish her position as "always right" and perceiving her husband as "always wrong," and Matthew had to stop simply being afraid of Cynthia's anger and examine why he was willing to keep looking like a screw-up. The pain of the process became clear as it dawned on them that they had spent many years simply following the dictates of their mutually compatible relationship template, thereby developing a one-sided view of each other's character. Becoming curious about why they had done this to each other began to generate the following type of repairing dramas:

Cynthia: "We just got a notice from our mortgage company that we are behind on our payments. You told me that you would take over paying the mortgage."

Matthew: "Oh, no! I forgot to send it in."

Cynthia: [*with great dismay and disgust*] "I can't believe you forgot! You promised that you would take care of this! What if we lose the house?"

[*At this point in their old recycling drama, Matthew is aware that Cynthia is justifiably angry at him for not following through on an agreement he had made to pay the mortgage, but he is conscious of not succumbing to his old fear of his wife's ire.*]

Matthew: "Now just a minute. You have every right to be mad at me for forgetting to send the payment this month, but we're not going to lose the house."

Cynthia: "How could you be so irresponsible? Do I have to do EVERYTHING?"

Matthew: "You know, Cynthia, I'm not going to let you label me as irresponsible again because I made one mistake." [*refusing the villain role*] "But I do think that we need to talk about why we just got into this old pattern again. I don't want you to feel like you have to do everything, and I really don't think that I'm the one who is making you feel that way."

Cynthia: [*sarcastically*] "Well, just who do you think is doing it then?"

Matthew: "We've learned that we both create our own feelings, so where are yours coming from?" [*asking to know her better*]

[*Cynthia is beginning to get her adult brain back, since Matthew has reminded her about the work they have been doing together to create repairing dramas.*]

Cynthia: [*after a moment of self-reflection*] "I did have to do everything in my childhood home, and that made me both angry and scared. I never had a chance to focus on what I needed as a child, because I was too busy taking care of everyone else in

Figure 11.2. Cynthia and Matthew's repairing drama

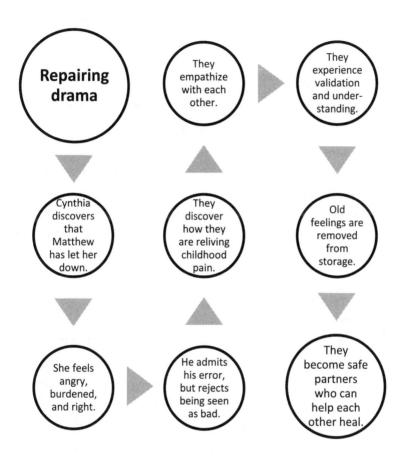

the family. And I was so scared that if I didn't do that, the whole place would just fall apart." [*Her childhood pain is now present.*] "When I feel like I can't count on you just like I couldn't count on them, I get so afraid again, but instead of feeling fear, I just get angry."

Matthew: "I can sure understand why my letting you down frightens you. I guess some part of my brain is still needing to relive shaming myself the way my parents did, instead of feeling angry at *them* for shaming me all the time."

Cynthia: "It is painful to watch you shame yourself, and it isn't going to change anything about the past. Let's work on finding ways to stop doing this to each other."

Matthew: "Good idea!"

In this repairing drama, Cynthia and Matthew relived anger, fear, and shame from the past, realized that these feelings were coming from childhood experiences with their parents, talked about their old losses and wounds, empathized with each other, and expressed validation and understanding that these feelings were very real to them in childhood. Repeating this type of repairing drama many times would lead to helping each other remove the old crazy-making emotions of fear and anger from storage for good.

Richard and Carol

During their six-month separation, Richard and Carol decided to keep working on their marriage. You read in the previous chapter how they prepared themselves for creating repairing dramas. Their recycling dramas followed a script in which she was the one who could directly express her anger and fears, while he could only show his emotions by acting out like a "sneaky" teenager. In truth he was terribly afraid that being married meant that Carol would control him, although he could not directly state this fear. Her nonconscious storage bin followed their mutual script by seeming controlling when she became afraid of losing him.

While they were negotiating a separation, they worked on transforming a recycling drama into a repairing drama around these emotions.

Richard: "I need to move to my own apartment so I can work on my art."

Carol: [*showing some anger and frustration*] "What? Why can't you work on your art at home?"

Richard: [*beginning to feel the fear of being controlled*] "Because you won't leave me alone."

Carol: [*more angry*] "I don't know what you're talking about!"

Richard: "Well, you come into the house after work and you want to talk to me right away, and I just want to be left alone."

Carol: [*working to stay safe*] "Why didn't you tell me that? I don't have to talk to you right away. All you have to do is tell me when you want to be left alone to paint." [*pleading*] "You don't have to move out to do that."

Richard: [*still afraid*] "I think I have to see what it feels like to be on my own."

Carol: [*Beginning to cry, she takes some time before responding.*] "I think I understand, since your parents never let you do your life your way, but it really scares me. We have to keep coming to therapy and have a plan for having dates with each other or something."

[*By this time in the treatment, Richard and Carol had already agreed that they were not interested in dating other people, which helped both of them feel safer with the separation.*]

Richard: "I know now that being with another woman isn't going to magically make me feel better. I'll keep coming to therapy with you, and we'll talk in a month or so about dating."

Carol: "You have to learn to tell me when you want something different than what I'm doing, rather than acting like you just have to go along because you're scared of me. That just creates a lot of distance between us. I don't expect you to do everything *my* way, like your family would have done to you. We have to work things out so that we are both getting what we need."

Richard: "I'll try, but my tendency is to just take care of myself."

Figure 11.3. Richard and Carol's repairing drama

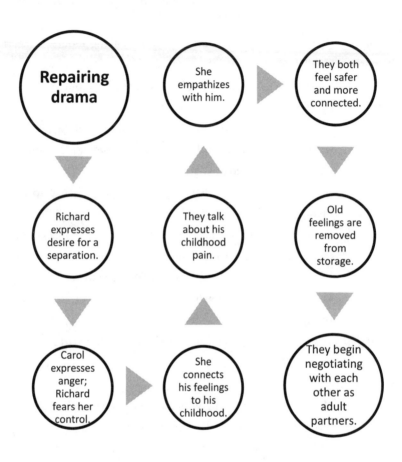

You can see how Richard has trouble here not falling back on the dictates of his original relationship template—that closeness and dependency are not safe. Carol is working hard to use safe communicating in order to set the stage for Richard to share more of himself with her.

This repairing drama was the first of many around Carol and Richard developing the ability to negotiate with each other. Richard's particular challenge was that he had to be aware of his emotions in order to be able to articulate his needs. He had become accustomed to avoiding his emotions. Since Carol was the "emoter" in their relationship, she could get perceived as too emotional—and therefore scary—thereby reinforcing Richard's pattern of distancing in relationships. In the past, openly expressing her emotions had gotten Carol demeaned, and shutting down his emotions had left Richard isolated. They were working hard to learn that taking responsibility for feeling and expressing their own emotions was necessary in order to safely negotiate a marriage.

CHAPTER 12

Metabolizing Emotions:
Hurt and Loneliness

As alluded to in the previous chapter, two of the earliest and most basic fears of human beings are annihilation and abandonment.[1] Both of these are about the fear of death. Annihilation is about being killed, and abandonment is about dying through being left alone.

The translation of these two primitive fears into more highly developed emotions are the feelings of hurt and loneliness. The infliction of emotional pain on us by a significant other leads to hurt feelings and confusion about why someone we need and love so much could be destructive to us. The greater the hurt, the more the nonconscious perceives that the other wishes to destroy. So hurt feelings are tied to the fear of being annihilated by a loved one.

The fear of abandonment underlies the emotions experienced when left alone by a loved one. Loneliness is not about simply being physically alone. Choosing to engage in solitary time can be quite enjoyable and essential to peace of mind. Feeling lonely arises when the aloneness is not by choice and is accompanied by fears of isolation and rejection. We can feel lonely in others' presence if we are not being adequately noticed, valued, or understood. Loneliness is experienced in an intimate relationship when one's important needs and feelings are being ignored or disregarded, whether the partners are physically together or not. If we feel forgotten and left to deal with difficulties on our own without the care and help we need, we feel lonely. If we don't experience that our presence brings joy to our loved ones, we feel lonely.

I have put these two emotions together in one chapter, because they are integrally tied to one another. Feeling hurt in a relationship often leads to feeling lonely. We feel alone with our emotions if they are not being treated with care. We feel abandoned in the relationship if our partners seem to choose to hurt us.

Hurt and loneliness will inevitably be relived in our intimate partnerships. The level of need that human beings experience in their most important relationships leaves us susceptible to feeling hurt and lonely. No one is perfect enough to guarantee that she or he will never hurt or emotionally abandon a loved one. And the hurt and loneliness that we experienced as too overwhelming in childhood will be stored in the nonconscious and relived in our adult partnerships.

Brad and Carolyn

The unmetabolized loneliness and abandonment in this couple's matching relationship template was palpable in every one of their recycling dramas, particularly when the subject of Carolyn's unresolved feelings about Brad's affair came up. Since Brad often felt compelled to repeat his childhood pattern of leaving in order to escape his uncomfortable feelings in the marriage, and Carolyn expected to be left because she saw herself as unlovable, it was a huge challenge for them to move toward repairing dramas in which no one got abandoned in the present.

Establishing safety in this marriage was going to be necessary in order to move toward repairing dramas. Both Carolyn and Brad felt as unsafe with each other as they had felt in their families of origin. Because they had become so hurtful to each other during their marriage, it was quite easy for them to blame each other for all of the emotions they were both feeling during their recycling dramas.

Figure 12.1. Brad and Carolyn's recycling victims and villains drama

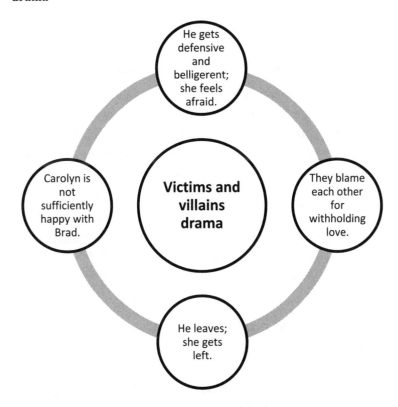

Remarkably, both Carolyn and Brad consistently expressed a mutual desire to keep their long marriage, although she frequently accused him of not really meaning it. They had both had plenty of chances to bail, but they had always reestablished their intent to stay together. Unfortunately, in spite of this stated level of commitment, they both did resort to threatening divorce at times, and their recycling dramas almost always included some form of Brad "running away from home."

It was a tremendous struggle for both Brad and Carolyn to give up the mutually compelling behaviors they had used to terrify, blame, and shame each other. They could spend hours—even days—trying to convince the other one to admit how badly he or she had acted and how justified their feelings were for their behaviors in the present. But they gradually began to get clear that acting out their victim and villain roles was going to destroy the marriage.

As Carolyn and Brad worked on being more safe with each other, he started to connect his need to escape from Carolyn with the pattern of jumping on his bicycle and riding off to anywhere to get away from his mother's crazy rants. But Carolyn was still stuck on blaming Brad for all of her fears of being left, because she remained unaware of the extent of her mother's abandonment. It was many months into their treatment before she admitted that her brother had expressed suspicions that their mother had had an affair during their youth. In fact, Carolyn had been forced into service taking care of the family when her mother was "unavailable." Having not yet consciously mourned the end of her childhood, Carolyn was determined to place all of her fears of being left on Brad's affair. Their recycling dramas had made it easy for her to blame him for all of her unmetabolized feelings of loneliness and abandonment.

The parents who had abandoned both Brad and Carolyn by failing to protect them from the developmental deficiencies of their mothers were, of course, their fathers. The extent of their abandonment was unbearable for either Carolyn or Brad to consciously feel, because idealizing the fathers had become necessary to avoid total despair in their childhoods.

Tackling these difficult old unmetabolized emotions in a repairing drama required Brad and Carolyn to take more responsibility for thinking before reacting and to assign their emotions to their childhoods.

[*Carolyn walks into the dining room as Brad is setting the table for a family dinner they're hosting.*]

Carolyn: "Oh. I was thinking of using a different table setting this time."

Brad: [*with frustration and some irritation in his voice*] "So, I did it wrong."

Carolyn: "I didn't say you did it wrong. I just wish you had asked me what I had in mind before you did it."

Brad: [*now feeling angry and hurt*] "You don't think I know how to set a table? I guess I shouldn't have tried to be helpful!"

Carolyn: "I didn't say that either. But you don't ever care about what I want before you just go ahead and do something."

[*Brad really wants to explode angrily for being accused of not caring, but he contains himself (thinking before reacting) long enough to realize that he is reliving the same pattern he experienced with his mother. He has to go to another room to calm himself down.*]

Carolyn: "Where are you going? You know I can't stand it when you walk away from me!"

[*Brad realizes that he is not responsible for Carolyn's anger and focuses on managing his own emotions. She is left alone to think about her own feelings. He comes back to her after a few minutes have elapsed and finds her in tears.*]

Carolyn: "Why do you always have to leave? It feels so awful to me!"

Brad: "I didn't leave this time; I just went to another room for a few minutes."

Carolyn: "But it feels the same to me."

Brad: "I know, and I'm sorry that it feels bad, but I am doing my best to stay safe." [*taking responsibility*]

[*Brad's use of the word "safe" reminds Carolyn of the preparations they have been working on for repairing dramas.*]

Carolyn: "I know, but I just panic so quickly about believing that you'll really leave me."

Brad: "Panic? I'm the one who panics when you tell me I don't care!"

[Labeling their feelings with the same word helps them stop and focus on taking responsibility for their own emotions. They take a few moments to get their adult brains back and become genuinely curious about what is going on with them.]

Carolyn: "I guess we both must be expecting something really awful to happen." *[reliving childhood trauma]* "We've been working on putting our feelings in the past where they belong. Mine must be about feeling left, and yours about being accused of not caring." *[wanting to know each other better]*

Brad: "Yeah, and those things really happened to us when we were kids."

Carolyn: "Well, I can see how your mom accused you of not caring, but I don't remember anybody leaving me but you."

[With this renewed recycling drama provocation from Carolyn, Brad has to work hard to think before reacting in order to get them back on the repairing track.]

Brad: "It's really painful to me that that was my role in our past, but I think your parents left you before I did." *[taking responsibility]*

Carolyn: "What are you talking about?" *[struggling with childhood pain]*

Brad: "Well, your dad was away for work a lot. And if your mom had really been there for you, you wouldn't have gotten abused by your neighbor."

[This statement by Brad hits Carolyn to the core of her childhood pain. She cries for a few moments before she can speak.]

Carolyn: "I've always seen the abuse as *my* fault."

Brad: "That's not true—you were just a little kid."

[Brad holds Carolyn while she cries.]

Carolyn: "Please tell me you won't leave me."

Brad: "I have no desire to leave you, but I also need for you to stop telling me I don't care, because that isn't true either."

Carolyn: "It just seems that way when you walk out."

Brad: "I'll try really hard to stop doing that. I just have to remember that you're not my mother." [*mourning the end of childhood*]

Carolyn: [*slightly chuckling*] "Thank God! And thank you for staying with me while I was hurting just now. I think I'm beginning to let myself see how much my mother didn't want to be a mother."

Figure 12.2. Brad and Carolyn's repairing drama

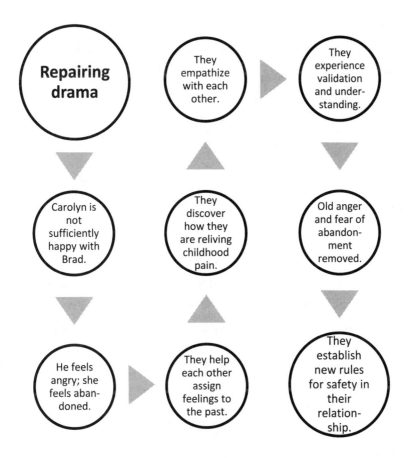

In this interaction, you can see how Brad and Carolyn struggled to stay on the repairing path, instead of getting back into a recycling drama. I point this out to emphasize that it takes conscious effort and difficult emotional risks to metabolize childhood pain. In this repairing drama, Carolyn and Brad are beginning to take the risk to deal with the abandonment of both their mothers and their fathers. They would need many more of these types of conversations to completely take the old fears of hurt and abandonment out of storage.

Charles and Kristine

Four years of waiting for Charles to make up his mind about being with her had certainly made Kristine feel alone and abandoned. Her conscious awareness of these emotions was a critical element of her role in the recycling dramas of the suffering that each of them had had to endure in their families of origin to atone for the shame of having needs. Even though both Charles and Kristine had been abandoned to loneliness for needing their parents in ways the parents couldn't manage, and then told that having to deal with life alone was virtuous, he had no awareness of these unmetabolized emotions.

So complete was Charles' denial of his lonely feelings in childhood that he had learned to idealize independence. Believing that he was choosing independence also served to keep him from feeling the shame of needing someone, thus keeping two emotional "birds" at bay with one "stone." On the other hand, Kristine was painfully aware of how lonely she had felt during the long course of the periods in their relationship when they were apart. She felt that she had waited patiently (suffered enough) while Charles got out of his second marriage and lived with her the agreed-upon period of time before he and Kristine could marry. She was angry and hurt at the beginning of their treatment that Charles was still dragging his feet about getting married. The roles that they were both playing in this standoff about moving toward marriage are clear in this recycling drama.

Figure 12.3. Charles and Kristine's recycling shame/reunion drama

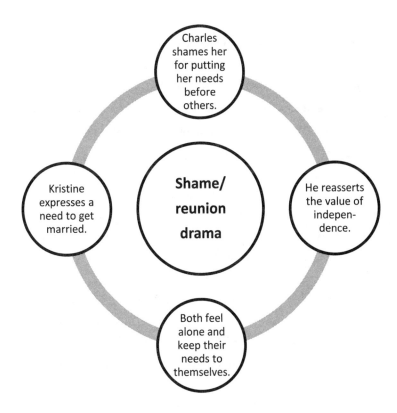

Kristine: "I thought you said you would be willing to set a date in May."

Charles: "No, we can't do it then. That's when Amy [*his daughter*] wants to get married."

Kristine: [*with disappointment in her voice*] "OK, so when then?"

Charles: "Well, then I have my trip to Montana. Then, it will be summer vacation, and I promised to do some things with Diane's [*ex-wife*] kids."

Kristine: [*beginning to cry*] "But you promised *me* that we would talk about getting married this fall. We've lived together long enough; I don't want to keep going this way."

Charles: "This is when I start to get really nervous about getting married. I've always had to do what everybody else wanted me to do or feel guilty if I don't. So it's just easier to be by myself."

How were they going to transition this into a repairing drama?

Charles and Kristine had tremendous desire and commitment to be together. Their relationship had weathered many storms already. They always treated each other with respect, and they were pretty good at taking responsibility for their own feelings and actions. So the lack of safety that both of them felt in their relationship was clearly based on past experiences with others. They mostly wanted to focus their fear of trusting on their past *marriages*, so much of their work toward repairing dramas required that they tackle the pain stored in those matching nonconscious storage bins about their childhoods. They had to become curious about why both of them were so doggedly independent, and they needed to cement the safety in their relationship by following through on their plans to marry.

So Kristine took the risk to momentarily feel her own pain in order to know Charles better.

Kristine: [*with genuine interest, not blame or anger*] "So you'd really rather be by yourself than with me?"

Charles: [*a bit exasperated*] "No, that's not what I meant!"

Kristine: "Then what did you mean?"

[*Charles has to stop to think, instead of just reacting. Kristine gives him plenty of time.*]

Charles: "I'm afraid that when we get married you will start dictating my life—telling me I can't take my trips to Montana and stuff."

Kristine: "I've never been like that with you. Why would I start now?"

Charles: "That's just what women do when they are in a family."

Kristine: [working to not get defensive and maintain genuine curiosity] "When has that happened to you before?"

Charles: "In both of my previous marriages."

Kristine: "I know that, but what about before that? Your mother seems pretty controlling to me."

Charles: [He laughs.] "That's an understatement! I *still* have to cater to her."

Kristine: "So you're afraid I'll turn into your mother."

Charles: "That's not a nice thought!"

Kristine: "No, but I can understand why you would be afraid of that." [empathizing]

[Both pause to let the unmetabolized emotions surface.]

Kristine: "Charles, there's probably nothing I can say to perfectly reassure you that I don't want to control your life, but I haven't been that way up to now. I've never minded that you take trips on your own or spend time with your own friends, and that won't change. We've always been respectful of each other's space."

Charles: "You're right, but why are you pressuring me to get married?"

Kristine: "I think I'm just following up on what we agreed to in the first place, and I'm taking responsibility finally for not continuing to passively suffer in this relationship."

Charles: "I don't want either one of us to suffer, but I'm having a hard time trusting that our relationship will stay good. I don't want to be by myself, but I don't want to lose myself to you, either."

[Charles takes some time to let old pain surface.]

Charles: "My mother taught me that it was my job to keep her happy.

I could tell you story after story from my childhood that ended in the message from her that it was wrong to go off and enjoy myself if it meant that she was left alone to take care of herself. She made sure that I 'suffered' for getting what I wanted if it made her feel bad. Even worse, she might act at first like it was OK for me to do my own thing, and then later she would make sure I knew that I had somehow abandoned her. So I learned that I couldn't trust what she told me. If you become my wife, part of me is scared that it will be the same—that you will expect me to keep you happy all the time, regardless of what I want, and then you'll act like the wounded woman who feels let down. It's a lose/lose situation for me."

Kristine: "I don't expect you to keep me happy—that's not your job. But I can see why you would worry that that would become your form of 'suffering' in our marriage." [*empathizing*]

[*He pauses, wanting to believe that his old type of suffering might be over. He realizes that he is going to have to risk reliving the emotions created by his relationship with his mother in order to have the life he has wanted with Kristine. He comes back to her within a couple of hours.*]

Charles: "I promise that I will let you know in a week when we can set a date."

Kristine: "And I promise that I have no interest in stealing your life away from you!"

And indeed, having successfully repeated this type of repairing drama in order to metabolize the loneliness that they had been reliving in their relationship, they did get married within a few months of this conversation.

Figure 12.4. Charles and Kristine's repairing drama

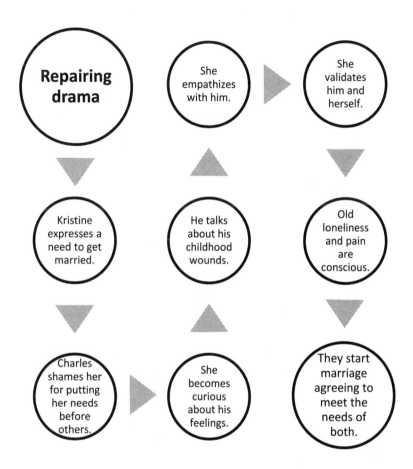

Richard and Carol

The victims and villains drama of affairs is created to make one partner look like the hurt*er* and one the hurt*ee*. The one inflicting the hurt can escape awareness of his or her own hurt feelings from the past, and the one being hurt in the marriage can quite easily attribute all of her or his hurt feelings to the present situation. Carol was certainly feeling hurt when Richard revealed his affair and wish to separate, but Richard's hurt was hiding behind his role as the "bad guy" for having cheated on her. Enacting the role of the hurter was familiar to his relationship template. He had been told by his family of origin that expressing his individuality was hurtful to them, so his hurting Carol was a way to keep from noticing that *he* was hurt by his parents' inability to let him grow up and become his own person.

Richard's compulsion to become involved with other women and eventually ask for a marital separation was also a recycling drama of loneliness. He imagined that the only way he could get his needs met was to be alone, and their separation obviously brought up feelings of loneliness for Carol. Living apart for six months while continuing to work on their relationship proved to be an extended repairing drama around the emotions of hurt and loneliness. Richard and Carol both learned to be present to what they were feeling and to own their internal experiences as coming from each of their nonconscious storage bins, instead of from their partner's behavior.

One of the repairing dramas that resulted from Carol and Richard continuing treatment during their separation went something like this:

Carol: "I was *so* hurt when I found out about your affair. I just couldn't believe that you would do that to me."

Richard: "I know, and I was confused about why I was doing it, too."

[*Both pause to tolerate the pain.*]

Richard: "It sounds stupid now, but I think that I might have been trying to get back at my family by hurting you." [*taking responsibility*] "It always seemed like you had to have things your way, just like them."

Carol: "I know that I was always the pushy one in our relationship, but your depression always kept you so stuck. You seemed to want me to take the lead in our relationship because you couldn't make up your mind about anything. I know now that my anxiety about your indecision was tapping into feelings that I didn't know my mother had about me. We both thought that my mother was so loving, but now I see that her love for me was seriously compromised by not getting over the death of her first husband. Finding that out in our therapy has hurt a lot." [*mourning the end of childhood*]

Richard: "I'm sorry that I've hurt you, too." [*taking responsibility*]

[*Both pause again to allow the pain.*]

Carol: "Thanks, but I'm concerned that you still don't get how much your family also hurt you in the past and continue to do it. You seem to sort of let me do all the anger toward them."

Richard: "Oh, I feel angry at them, but it doesn't do much good to tell *them*. I want to believe that I just gave up on them a long time ago, instead of feeling hurt."

Carol: "Well, I'm going to work on giving you more room to feel your own emotions instead of being the one to do them for both of us. The more we can both talk about how we feel, the less likely it will be that we will repeat all of the old patterns that hurt each other so much."

In another repairing drama, Richard and Carol were able to use what they had learned about themselves as they negotiated an end to their separation.

Richard: "I think that in order for me to feel comfortable with living together again, we're going to have to find a different house. I don't have enough space in the old house."

Carol: "That's fine with me. I've learned that your need for space has nothing to do with me. It used to make me feel abandoned, like the way it felt with my mother. But now I know it's just about *your* fear of being crowded by me and my needs. But we'll have to find somewhere that really works for both of us. Like I still want us to have a family, so it would have to be big

Figure 12.5. Richard and Carol's repairing drama

enough for your space and for kids."

Richard: "I don't know about kids yet." [*He is beginning to feel a bit panicked, but he is speaking up for himself without pulling away.*] "But I'm willing to keep talking about it and to make sure that we have a place big enough."

Carol: [*tearfully*] "I'm just glad that you're ready to get back together. I think that we've both learned a lot about how to honor our own feelings and still get what we need from each other."

CHAPTER 13

Metabolizing Emotions: Shame

As stated earlier, shame is a universal emotion of all humans that accompanies our growing awareness that we are not "all good." We experience shame when we see the disapproval of important people in our lives and fear being shunned by them. There is no way to escape the emotion of shame in our lives, and the mastery of this emotion is a critical piece of becoming a successful, happy adult.

Our experience of shame is shaped by the reactions of our significant others. If our families do not react to a particular behavior with disapproval, then repeating that behavior will not arouse shame. For example, some families or cultures might see eating with your hands as shameful, whereas in other families or cultures it might be seen as normal. Also, our parents may have differing levels of tolerance for the behaviors they regard as wrong. If their tolerance is low, they may emotionally frighten or overly humiliate a child, leading to greater levels of unmetabolized shame for the child. If their tolerance is higher, they may be capable of helping their children learn to metabolize normal shame without unnecessary trauma.

Children whose parents do not adequately disapprove at the appropriate moments will develop a sense of self that does not contain the mastery of shame. These children become the self-centered, overly entitled adults that we sometimes refer to as narcissists. In contrast, children whose brains are overwhelmed with too much shame too often will develop an experience of self with others in which they are victims of the dictates of others. Most of us fall somewhere in the middle of these two extremes. Again, the point is that the ability to feel and overcome shame is essential to normal adult mental health.[1]

I want to make the important point here that the emotion of shame is not limited to the parts of the body below the waist. It is not just about sexual or elimination behaviors, although those may be some of the first areas that draw our parents' disapproval. We humans experience shame with any behavior that we have been taught is wrong or bad. Anything we do that has the potential of making us feel like a bad person can evoke shame.

Unfortunately, in many recycling dramas the shameful behavior truly is bad, such as lying, abuse, or having an affair. This makes the preparation for repairing dramas all the more difficult and all the more painful. Establishing safety in a relationship that has been repeating these types of dramas can take a long time, with careful attention to all four aspects of safety shown in Figure 8.1.

Quite often in marriages, the way that unmetabolized shame in both partners shows up in recycling dramas is for one partner to have the shameful behavior, while the other looks on with innocent disdain.[2] I will emphasize again, *both* partners have unmetabolized shame in their nonconscious storage bins, and *both* brains contain the belief that the bad behavior deserves punishment. So this must be relived with a recycling drama in which one does the bad behavior and the other does the punishing. Then the one with the shameful behavior has to create a reunion with the punishing or victimized spouse that resembles the reunions in both of their childhoods.

Cynthia and Matthew

The shame/reunion dramas that you read about in chapter 6 are the venue through which couples relive their unmetabolized shame. As they argued about his supposed irresponsibility, Matthew and Cynthia were recycling a mutual shame/reunion drama that required him to be the carrier of all the shame. This was a repetition of the same role Matthew had been forced into in his family of origin. His father was a prominent physician who had the good performer niche sewn up. Within his family system, Matthew was not permitted to be seen as competent; instead, he was derided for being a "goofball," and he never performed to his intellectual potential as a student. In the course of his marriage to Cynthia, he had acted out his

Figure 13.1. Cynthia and Matthew's recycling shame/reunion drama

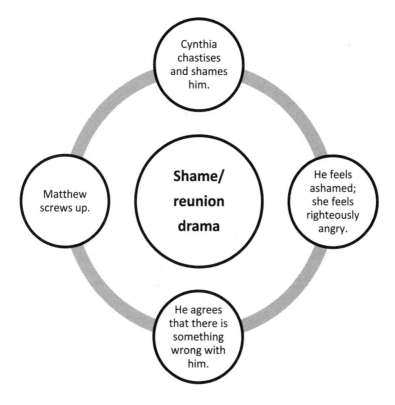

incompetence through financially failing in his own medical practice and occasionally threatening their personal finances by forgetting to take care of some important task he had agreed to do.

Whenever Cynthia chastised Matthew for messing up, the reunion in the marriage was created by Matthew agreeing to Cynthia's "discipline." Through her righteous indignation, Cynthia could circumvent conscious awareness of her own shameful feelings and therefore repeat the avoidance of shame that had been necessary in her family of origin. She had been called upon to function as an overadapted, adultlike child by developmentally deficient parents who needed her to keep order in a chaotic household. As the good child that the family needed to perform parental tasks, she had been forced into being the one who controlled others with shame but never felt her own.

Taking responsibility for behaving more safely in the relationship allowed Matthew and Cynthia to see that the shameful behaviors that they were exhibiting with each other were a repetition of their childhood roles instead of their true natures. They began to see that they had been equally unsafe to each other and to the relationship, instead of viewing only Matthew as unsafe. Cynthia took the risk to notice how she had been mistreating Matthew with her critical tirades, and he took the risk to become genuinely curious about why he kept making himself look and feel so inadequate.

The first outcome of confronting their mutual shame/reunion drama was Matthew's relief that he didn't have to accept Cynthia's discipline anymore. Instead—as you read in their repairing drama in chapter 11—Matthew began to stand up for himself and recognize that his supposed incompetence was the reliving of shame from his childhood. He began to enjoy the competence as a husband, father, and professional that he had denied himself in order to participate in the old dramas. Cynthia began to see how her conceptualizations of Matthew's character were a half-baked notion of him based on mutual repetitions of their childhood shame/reunion dramas. She began to rely on him more and relinquish her parental position in the marriage. An interesting outcome of this shift was that she became anxious that she would lose her previous sense of being "the competent one." She gradually developed the capacity to see that her previous false sense of competence—more accurately superiority—was in fact her part of the old reunions that she could relinquish in repairing dramas.

Cynthia: "My family is falling apart again and expecting me to come fix things. Don't they understand how much it costs for me to keep flying down there and that I have a life of my own to deal with here?" [*showing anger and fatigue*]

Matthew: "You know that the answer to both of those questions is NO."

Cynthia: "If I don't go, everything will go to pieces down there, and if I do go, everything will fall apart here. So I'm a failure either way." [*unmetabolized shame*]

Matthew: "What do you mean everything will fall apart here?" [*starting to get annoyed but remembering how to stay safe*] "We've been through this. It's really old business for you to start thinking again that you can't count on me, but I understand that you're probably feeling really stressed and resorting to old beliefs about me." [*empathizing*]

[*Cynthia pauses to reflect on all of the new repairing dramas they have been constructing together.*]

Cynthia: "I'm sorry; I guess it's just sort of new for me to believe I can count on you and that I'm not alone with this problem." [*She pauses, and old pain begins to surface.*] "I have always felt so ashamed of my family. My brother was always being so crazy all the time, and my parents always behaved like they didn't know what to do about anything. They have always looked to me for all of the answers, and I had to act like I had them. Now they want me to do it again!"

Matthew: "Do you know how many times you used the word 'always' just now?"

[*They both laugh.*]

Matthew: "We *can* stop the 'always,' you know. You don't have to go down there. Your younger brother lives there; let him handle it."

Figure 13.2. Cynthia and Matthew's repairing drama

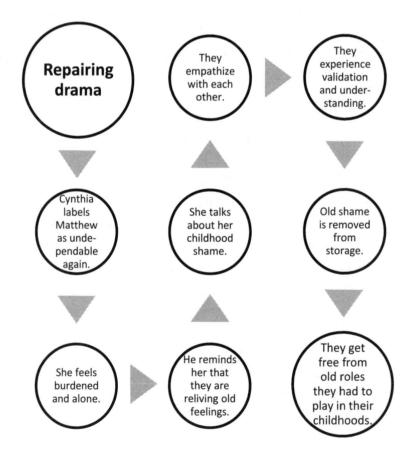

Cynthia: "I guess I've always (that word again) just seen him as the little kid that I had to protect. But he's a grown-up and a minister, and I think that my parents actually do trust him."

Matthew: "We both know what it's like to come from such a dysfunctional family. Let's put our efforts into being there for each other."

Cynthia: "You're right. I'm not going! Thanks for helping me see it this way."

Brad and Carolyn

Carolyn: "I can't stop thinking about what you did to me when you had your affair."

Brad: "I know that I really hurt you, but that was twenty years ago."

Carolyn: "I still have feelings about it, and I don't think that you understand yet how bad it was for me. I felt *so* abandoned." [*beginning to cry*]

Brad: "We've been over this a thousand times. You're right—what I did to you was really awful, but I've apologized to you over and over. Besides, I chose to be with you in the end."

Carolyn: "I know, but I still don't feel really heard by you."

Brad: [*starting to get frustrated*] "What do you mean I haven't heard you? I have listened to you for hours at a time tell me how angry and hurt you still are."

Carolyn: "You just don't understand how alone I felt. You confirmed how unlovable I am." [*in a high-pitched voice and sobbing*] "How could you do that to me if you love me? I think that you just don't love me!"

Brad: [*in a pleading tone*] "That isn't true. I *do* love you."

Carolyn: "No, you don't. You couldn't possibly love me and do the things you've done."

[*Carolyn continues for several more minutes recounting all of the ways that Brad has been unloving.*]

Brad: [*Now feeling exasperated and desperate, he answers with an angry, clipped, sarcastic tone.*] "OK, you're right. I don't love you! Are you happy now?"

This type of recycling shame/reunion drama occurred hundreds of times in this marriage. Carolyn could not stop reliving how unloved she felt when Brad had his affair, and she would wear him down with the list of how bad he had been to her until his nonconscious complied by shaming himself with hurting her feelings exactly the same way again. Their childhood reunions had required that they keep their upset feelings to themselves, so their shame/reunion drama had to end this same way.

Figure 13.3. Brad and Carolyn's recycling shame/reunion drama

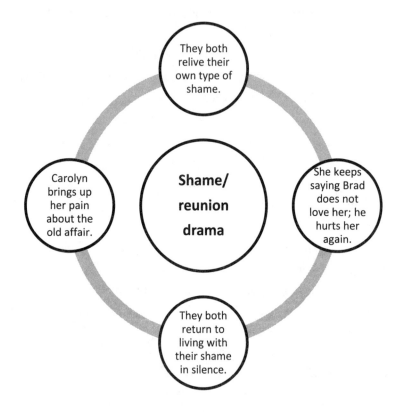

Their nonconscious storage bins had constructed the perfect recycling drama for them to relive the immense amount of shame that they both still carried from their childhoods.

In order to make the transition to a repairing drama, both Carolyn and Brad would have to take on the difficult task of taking responsibility for their own shameful feelings and the even more painful task of feeling how their parents had shamed them. Unfortunately for Brad, their nonconscious storage bins had assigned him the role of enacting most of the shameful behaviors. This is how he had been the nonconscious "sacrificial lamb" in their marriage to protect Carolyn from being conscious of all the shame she carried from childhood.

Let's return to their scripted interaction above and see how they made the transition.

Carolyn: "You just don't understand how alone I felt. You confirmed how unlovable I am." [*in a high-pitched voice and sobbing*] "How could you do that to me if you love me? I think that you just don't love me!"

Brad: [*in a pleading tone*] "That isn't true. I *do* love you."

Carolyn: "No, you don't. You couldn't possibly love me and do the things you've done."

[*Carolyn struggles to stop herself from recounting all of the ways that Brad has been unloving. They both fall silent in order to stop the blaming and tolerate their own pain. The tone in Brad's voice reminds Carolyn how much it hurts him to be accused of not caring.*]

Carolyn: [*beginning to cry*] "Can you understand how unworthy and unlovable I felt when you were having your affair?" [*asking to be known better*]

Brad: [*tolerating his own pain*] "I think I can. Can you understand how awful I feel about myself for doing that to you?" [*Now he is crying.*] "It makes me crazy to think about how I made you feel unloved, when all I've really wanted to do is show you how much I love you. My mother wouldn't ever let me do that!"

[*They have to pause again. This is very hard.*]

Brad: "I'd give anything to convince you that you're lovable."

[*Carolyn has calmed down and gotten her adult brain back.*]

Carolyn: "I wish you could, but you can't." [*tolerating her pain and mourning childhood loss*]

Brad: "I know."

Carolyn: "So—what are we going to do?"

<u>Figure 13.4.</u> Brad and Carolyn's repairing drama

Brad: "I think right now we just have to work on being safe."

Carolyn: "And talking more about how our parents made us feel bad about ourselves. That's going to take a long time."

Brad: "That's OK with me, as long as we take some breaks to have some fun."

Carolyn: [*She smiles.*] "OK."

Charles and Kristine

The fact that Charles and Kristine could treat each other with respect and take responsibility for their own behaviors and feelings helped them move out of their dramas around avoiding marriage and recycling

Figure 13.5. Charles and Kristine's recycling shame/reunion drama

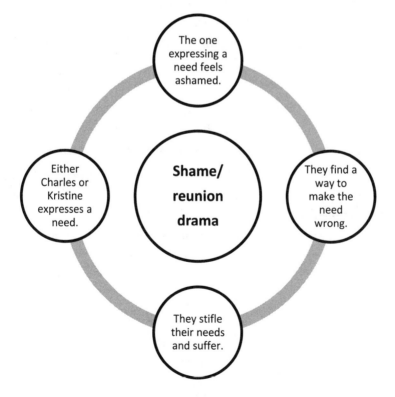

The one expressing a need feels ashamed.

Either Charles or Kristine expresses a need.

Shame/
reunion
drama

They find a way to make the need wrong.

They stifle their needs and suffer.

loneliness relatively early in their treatment with me. Getting married created the safety that their nonconscious storage bins needed to tackle their recycling dramas about shame. As you read before in chapter 6, Charles and Kristine could be made to feel that they were bad people for simply expressing normal human needs. They wanted to be together and enjoy their lives, but their own recycling dramas kept injecting suffering to interrupt their joy. They literally felt ashamed for wanting to be happy, perceiving what others outside their relationship needed from them as always more important and therefore demanding priority.

Both Kristine and Charles openly expressed a strong desire to heal their mutual shame and thereby eliminate the need to repeat the shame/reunion dramas that had previously caused them so much pain. Because they could both take responsibility for feeling their own shame, their task in preparing for repairing dramas boiled down to talking about what it would take to help them relinquish the self-imposed suffering that was their mutual path to reunions. They were quite aware that this would be no easy task and that they would inevitably struggle with the fear that rejecting suffering in favor of their own appropriate needs would lead to losing connection.

You read in chapter 6 the recycling drama that Kristine and Charles had created around the chronic problems that she had with her eyes, which seemed to be connected to her job. Although she had agreed to retire, she felt ashamed about largely depending on Charles to support them financially and afraid that she did not have enough money in her retirement to be able to pay her own way for her needs. In order to deal with her shame around Charles being willing to help her financially, Kristine had to confront painful truths about her family's idealization of independence.

Charles: [*on arriving home after work*] "Did you enjoy your day today?"
Kristine: "Not really. I can't stop worrying about money."
Charles: "We've been over this. I have plenty of money to take care of both of us."

Kristine: "I know, but it just doesn't seem right for me to depend on you that way."

Charles: "Why not? I'm happy to do it."

Kristine: "I know you've said that, but I worry that you will resent me some day."

Charles: "Where does that idea come from?" [*wanting to know her better*]

[*Kristine stops and puts effort into resisting blaming their present behavior for her emotions.*]

Kristine: "My father always told all of us that we should be able to pay our own way, and I was a woman of the sixties. I was always determined to have my own money. It's a good thing I did, since my ex was worthless when it came to supporting us!"

Charles: "I remember how you were struggling when you were married to him, and even after, he didn't keep up with child support."

Kristine: "So, see; I learned that being independent is really better."

Charles: "I know—we've both had that issue." [*He smiles playfully.*]

[*They pause to let other old emotions surface.*]

Kristine: "You know, I think that my parents taught all of us kids really early that being independent was the right way to be. How else were they going to deal with five kids? Since the twins came along when I was only two, I must have had to feel really proud of myself for being independent, instead of noticing that my mother wasn't available to me. Maybe your willingness to help me brings up some old pain that I don't want to face." [*mourning the end of childhood*]

Charles: "I can see how it would, but I want us to be able to enjoy our lives together, and I couldn't see how that was going to happen with you in physical pain all the time."

Kristine: [*sarcastically*] "You mean the 'suffering twins'? Why should we enjoy ourselves?" [*She laughs, and then realizes that she has*

Figure 13.6. Charles and Kristine's repairing drama

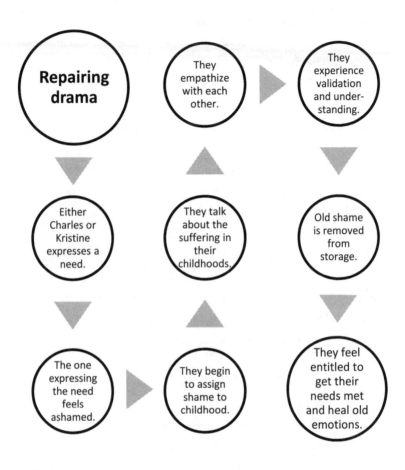

used the word *"twins." Gasping with surprise at herself, she says . . .*] "I must have some resentment about my twin brothers taking all of our mother's attention. I never knew."

Charles: "It makes sense to me that you would, but you would have had to feel ashamed of that resentment. The way these old feelings come out is remarkable to me. You're not afraid of *my* resentment—you've been afraid of your own."

CHAPTER 14

Metabolizing Emotions: Despair

I have been working with human beings long enough to know that feeling helpless is one of the worst emotions we can experience, and we will go to great lengths to avoid this horrible feeling. The panic accompanying helplessness derives from the fear of not being able to continue our lives. When we believe we are in a situation in which we literally cannot stop or escape danger or we are being repeatedly blocked from having important needs met, we feel the powerlessness of the victim. Prolonged inability to help ourselves leads to despair, expressed in the words, "This is hopeless."

Children who do not experience their parents as responsive to their needs will likely feel despair. With every episode in which children feel helpless to impact their parents in ways necessary to their survival or well-being, the despair increases. The play for attention and care becomes desperate until repeated failures to reach the parents results in permanently succumbing to hopelessness.

Couples who are reliving despair must create recycling dramas in which they experience each other as disregarding important needs and running roughshod over the emotional safety of the other. They come into treatment saying literally or figuratively, "You've *got* to make him/her STOP!" or "I can't take this anymore." Or any number of ways to say that they are at the end of their rope. They are making a desperate plea for help, because to them the situation has gotten too painful to bear, and they no longer know what to do to make it better.

In order to relive despair, they must eventually experience powerlessness to impact their partner's behavior or emotions, and they come to see each other as uncaring and unavailable to hear what their partner has to say. If their inabilities to impact each other continue long enough, they experience their relationship as impossible to improve, and they relive the despair of children whose parents were never going to develop the capacity to care for them the way they needed to be.

An intriguing aspect of the reliving of despair is that couples usually consciously assign the "never" word to the future. The hopeless feelings tend to be about what will never happen in the time to come. There is denial that the only time in our lives that is truly hopeless is the past. Changing the past is impossible, but we all try to do precisely that in our recycling dramas. Attempting to change the past through the present or future will by definition lead to the reliving of despair, so the mourning of the loss of childhood is a particularly important step toward mutually creating repairing dramas around this critically important unmetabolized emotion. For couples to be able to help each other metabolize despair, they must consciously recognize that the truly hopeless situation was a done deal long before they knew each other.

Cynthia and Matthew

When Cynthia and Matthew began couples treatment, they were already in a state of despair. They had come to believe that their marriage probably couldn't be saved and that divorce might be their only option, even though they both openly expressed a desire to keep the marriage.

In previous descriptions of this couple's relationship, you have seen how each of them defined their desperate positions in the marriage. Cynthia experienced herself as having to do everything because she couldn't depend on Matthew, and thus she felt overwhelmed and overburdened in their relationship. Her role in their recycling dramas called for her to repeatedly beg, cajole, or scold Matthew as a means of trying to get him to understand how burdened she felt and thus motivate him to change his behavior. Of course, it never worked. Matthew desperately wanted to stop messing up, thereby quelling Cynthia's anger at him and allowing him to feel better about himself, but his role in their recycling dramas dictated that he would endlessly reexperience the pain of repeated inadequacy and shame.

Figure 14.1. Cynthia and Matthew's recycling victims and villains drama

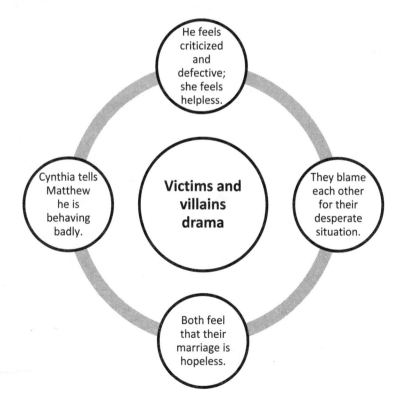

Out of their matching nonconscious storage bins had come these roles that could keep them feeling the same way they did as children. The unmetabolized despair that they were experiencing in their marriage was completely valid and real in their childhoods. Through her parents' developmental deficiencies, Cynthia had been forced into having to take on adult-level responsibilities that indeed would be overwhelming and overburdening to any child. And Matthew's brain compelled him to experience in his marriage the reliving of the way his father had treated him. He couldn't stop the old pattern until he was ready to feel how hopeless it was that he would have ever seen his father look at him with pride.

In order to change their recycling dramas about despair into repairing dramas, Matthew and Cynthia had to remind each other about the safety necessary to mourn their childhood losses and create an atmosphere of empathy in order to metabolize the old, crazy-making feelings.

Cynthia: "You've got to stop being so irrational! You're driving me crazy! There must be something wrong with your meds."

Matthew: [*refusing the villain role*] "I don't know what you're talking about, and I don't appreciate your talking about 'my meds' to remind me that I'm the one with 'the problem.'"

Cynthia: "You're ranting and raving at everybody around here about not doing what they're supposed to do, and you're the one who's acting irresponsible again."

Matthew: "I am not!"

Cynthia: "Yes, you are; you're being very unsafe!"

[*That word seems to be the trigger that helps both of them interrupt their angry tirades.*]

Matthew: [*becoming curious*] "What are we doing here? Why are we getting into this place again?"

Cynthia: [*beginning to calm herself and trying to stop feeling victimized*] "I don't know, but I feel that desperate feeling again when you won't stop."

Matthew: "When I won't stop what?"

Cynthia: "You've been so angry and irritable. What's going on with you?" [*wanting to know him better*]

[*Matthew takes time to think and access his own emotions before speaking. He had been seriously considering changing careers.*]

Matthew: "I think I'm just really nervous about giving up being a doctor. I think I'm afraid that I'll fail and then we won't have enough money. Then I will have let you down, exactly like you tell me I do, and you can think I'm a failure, just like my father did."

Cynthia: "I do get worried when you get so upset and seem to be denying reality. That's what my mother always did when my crazy brother would act out of control. It was clear to everyone else that he wasn't normal, but she didn't want to see it, so he kept wreaking havoc in our home. Even after he got convicted of assault and sent to prison, my mother refused to believe that he did it. *I* am the one who has had to stay engaged in his problems—not my parents."

Matthew: [*seeming subdued*] "I guess I must remind you of your brother sometimes."

Cynthia: "Oh, no! Do I really make you feel that bad?" [*She seems genuinely horrified at the idea.*] "I'm sorry. I think that I just start getting frightened and feeling sorry for myself when you get wound up about something, and then I start getting into those old thoughts about all of our problems being your fault. It's so much easier to blame you for everything than to remember how I was victimized as a kid."

Matthew: "I feel the same way. We can both get into desperate thinking about today instead of remembering to make each other feel safe by putting the losses in the past."

[*The conversation ends in quiet reflection.*]

Figure 14.2. Cynthia and Matthew's repairing drama

Karen and Bob

It seems pretty clear to me that resorting to domestic violence is an act of desperation. It certainly was in the marriage of Karen and Bob. Neither one of them was inherently a violent person, but they both felt desperate to be heard by the other. Karen was the one who called the police, and she was shocked and dismayed when they followed through with the accepted procedure of putting both her and Bob in jail. They were both feeling enraged, terrified, hurt, and hopeless by the time they got to my office. And you have already read about how driven both of them were to establish their own innocence in their recycling dramas.

Figure 14.3. Karen and Bob's recycling competition drama

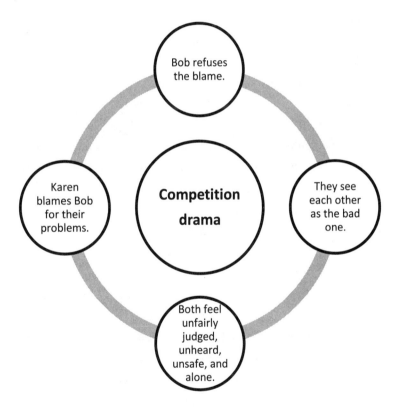

Both Bob and Karen were in hopeless situations as children. Since they both had one parent whose stunted development resulted in supremely self-centered and dangerous behaviors and one parent who seemed too weak to intervene, Karen and Bob were raised in families

where their needs were never going to be met. So they had no choice but to relive this desperate situation in their marriage.

The great challenge in preparing Bob and Karen for repairing dramas was seeing if they could work toward assuring safety in their relationship. They both expressed a strong commitment to keeping their marriage, so that was a good start. But in every other way their marriage had become highly unsafe to both of them. Their reciprocal roles in the recycling dramas were often to see themselves as the innocent victims of the other's bad behavior—an understandable repetition of having been true victims as children. It was extremely difficult for both of them to relinquish the victim role that they strongly wanted to keep reliving as a way to avoid mourning the permanent loss of a normal childhood. In particular, Karen was driven to unload all of the rage and terror that she had felt toward her abusive father onto Bob. She struggled over and over to understand that labeling Bob as the villain in the marriage was just as unsafe to him as feeling like the victim was to her.

Their ongoing bickering about which of them was to blame for starting an argument fueled the mutually held belief that their partner was the source of their pain. In fact, Bob's behavior in the marriage had been more obviously dangerous than Karen's in many instances. He was the one with the substance abuse and mood problems. But he also frequently apologized to Karen with heartfelt regret for his transgressions in the marriage. He often felt frustrated while attempting to get Karen to hear and value his thoughts and feelings about any number of topics. When his frustration erupted into anger at her, she always felt justified in perceiving him as being as dangerous as her father had been and then believing that all of her fear and anger was based on Bob's behavior in the present, instead of a repetition of her childhood terror.

Both Karen and Bob had major difficulties taking responsibility for their own thoughts, feelings, and actions. It took many months of work together for them to begin to develop an understanding that they couldn't "make" each other feel or do anything. As they learned about their nonconsciously constructed recycling dramas, Bob got clear that he wasn't simply a bad husband who had no control over himself. But he struggled to give up his need to see Karen as simply self-centered, like his mother. Their many rounds of trying to be heard and understood by each other culminated in the following long repairing drama, which ended up addressing many unmetabolized emotions.

Bob is, once again, trying to express his thoughts and feelings about something important, providing the perfect script for the reliving of despair.

Karen: "You're scaring me again with your anger. You always have to have everything your way."

Bob: "I'm not angry. All I did was disagree with you." [*taking responsibility*]

Karen: "No, you're trying to control me again. You always start a fight. I was just trying to say what I want, and you have to get all upset. I don't know why you have to be so unreasonable!"

Bob: "I'm not being unreasonable. I'm just trying to get you to hear what I think about this!"

Karen: "I don't think I can do this. I didn't do anything wrong, and you're yelling at me!"

Bob: "Fine. If you can't give up seeing me as the bad guy all the time, I'm not safe with you. I've already taken our motor home to a space a little ways from our house. I'm going to go stay there for a couple of weeks while you think about whether you can stop blaming me for starting all the fights. I don't want to lose our marriage, but I'm not going to take all the blame anymore." [*refusing the villain role*]

Karen: [*feeling somewhat panicked*] "No! Please don't do that!"

Bob: "I have to. We've got to stop this pattern, or we'll end up getting a divorce."

[*Bob follows through on living in their motor home for a couple of weeks, but he and Karen continue to talk.*]

Karen: [*with desperation in her eyes and voice*] "You've been gone for almost two weeks now. Are you ever coming back home?"

Bob: "Not until I know that you can stop blaming me for all of our problems."

Karen: "I'm just trying to get you to admit your faults."

Bob: "I've admitted my faults many times, and it's never enough for you. I mean it. If you can't stop blaming me for everything, we're done." [*He pauses and looks very sad.*] "I knew it would come to this."

[*Karen begins to cry and feel panicked. She is almost hyperventilating.*]

Karen: "I can't stand the thought of losing our marriage! That isn't what I want at all!"

Bob: "I don't want that either, but we can't keep acting like one of us is the bad guy. The bad guys are in our past. We have to let them go." [*mourning the end of childhood*]

Karen: [*sobbing*] "I can't! There was so much pain, and you just don't understand how bad it was."

Bob: "Actually, I think I know exactly how bad it was, but you keep pushing me away, so I can't help you with your feelings about your family. We can't help *each other*, and I really want to be able to do that." [*tolerating the pain*]

[*Living alone with her childhood pain for three more days creates a remarkable shift within Karen. She has never considered that she might really lose her marriage if she doesn't stop painting Bob as the villain. He has been able to tolerate the presence of his own despair that was connected to permanently losing his family in childhood so that he doesn't give in to Karen's panic. She approaches Bob again . . .*]

Karen: "I'm sorry. You're right." [*taking responsibility*] "I can't keep making you the bad guy." [*stopping the blaming*] "The bad guys are our parents for making our childhoods so unsafe. I do want us to be able to help each other with our feelings from childhood, and we have to be safe to do that."

Bob: [*seeming a bit shocked*] "You really mean that?"

Karen: "Yes, I do. Looking at the prospect of losing you forever sort of brought me to my senses. I know that we have been talking in therapy about giving up the victims and villains thing, but I couldn't imagine that you were going to get away with having hurt me so much. And then it finally struck me how much I had been bringing my childhood past into our marriage. My *father* got away with it, and he still does! But even if he gets held accountable, it doesn't change how much he has hurt all of us. I think I finally see—the damage has been done, and it doesn't do any good to keep damaging our marriage." [*mourning the end of childhood*]

Bob: "You're so right. I didn't want to lose our marriage either, but I didn't want to keep it the way it was."

Karen: "If I can promise that it will be different, will you move back home?"

Bob: "Gladly, and I'll be different too."

And they did act differently in the marriage from that day on. Being on the brink of recycling their hopelessness by losing their marriage propelled them into a repairing drama that changed their lives. Putting the old anger, fear, hurt, loneliness, and despair where it belonged in the past helped them move on and become each other's best healers.

Figure 14.4. Karen and Bob's repairing drama

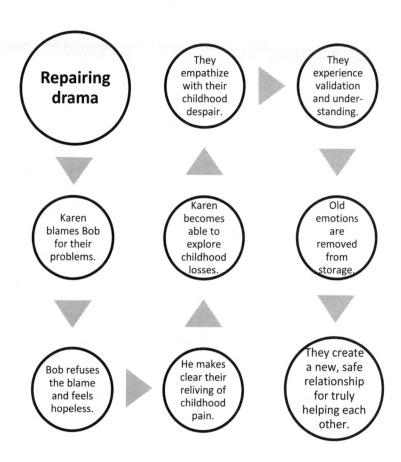

Richard and Carol

As you already know, Richard and Carol also had to live through a marital separation to relive the unmetabolized emotion of despair. Richard had to get to the point of believing that his marriage was hopeless, and Carol had to experience the hopelessness of watching her husband seem to give up on the marriage. At the beginning of their separation, neither one of them knew that the hopelessness they were recycling was about the relationships with their families of origin.

METABOLIZING EMOTIONS: DESPAIR

As Carol and Richard progressed in their treatment during their separation, they created together a safe place to explore the painful feelings associated with despair. You read in chapter 12 one of their repairing dramas around negotiating the end to their separation in which Carol brought up the subject of having their own children. She approaches this difficult subject again:

Carol: "I want us to talk again about having children."

Richard: "I told you that I don't want to think about that yet."

Carol: "But I need to talk about it. I'm not getting any younger, and these health issues I've been having could interfere with getting pregnant eventually. If we're going to have kids, we probably have to do it sooner rather than later."

Richard: "I'm feeling controlled again. The idea of becoming a parent makes me panic. I don't want that level of responsibility, and I don't want my own kid to experience not being wanted, like I felt." [*taking responsibility for his own feelings*]

Carol: [*beginning to cry*] "But I really want to be a mother."

Richard: "This is hopeless. You really want to have children, and I really don't. I can't see any way this can work out."

[*They are both quiet as Carol cries and Richard works to deal with his own desperate panic about feeling forced into parenthood. He decides to focus on trying to understand Carol's feelings.*]

Richard: "Why is having kids so important to you?" [*wanting to know her better*]

Carol: [*working to manage her own emotions*] "I've just assumed that's a natural thing, so I haven't given it much thought. My parents wanted children."

Richard: "Are you sure about that?"

[*Carol is struggling to think before automatically reacting in defense of her parents. She is trying to tolerate some kind of old pain that is beginning to surface.*]

Carol: "I'm sure that my father did, but something inside is telling me that maybe my mother only agreed to have me for him." [*The tears flow again.*] "There was some reason that I always felt this pressure to see her as so perfectly loving—maybe it's because she really wasn't. She tried, but since my older sister was the child of her first husband that she loved so much, I couldn't ever measure up."

Richard: "So you want to prove that you can be a better mother than she was to you?"

Carol: [*pensively experiencing her own childhood despair*] "I never would have thought that, but when you say it, it sounds right."

[*They pause to maintain safety.*]

Carol: [*Another idea about herself occurs to her.*] "You know, I probably also want you to *want* to be a parent, like that would fix something about my past." [*mourning the end of childhood*]

Richard: "Right now the thought of becoming a father scares me. Children are so dependent on you, and I'm just not sure I could be there for them—particularly with my depression and all that we've been going through. I don't know that I would have the energy, and I don't want to be getting angry at my own kids all the time, like my family did to me." [*taking responsibility*]

Carol: "No; that wouldn't be good." [*another pause*] "I guess I just want us to be able to keep talking about it."

Richard: "OK. I know that this is important to you, but you can't be pressuring me about it, like you tend to do."

Carol: "I know; that wouldn't be safe, but it's also not safe to think of this as a hopeless deal-breaker in our marriage."

Richard: "You're right."

Figure 14.5. Richard and Carol's repairing drama

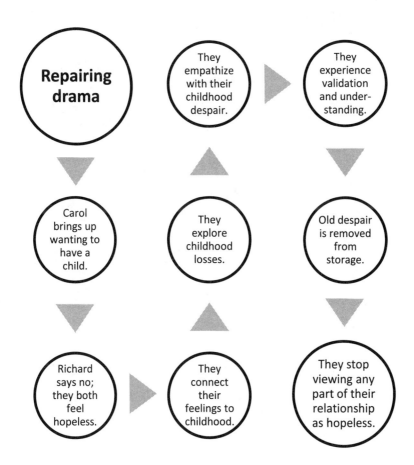

CHAPTER 15

Metabolizing Emotions: Sorrow

We all know that loss is one of those universal human experiences that is part of everyone's normal life.[1] It is an experience that we will have many times during our lives, and it must be mastered in order to avoid succumbing to despair. We begin life with the loss of the safety and warmth of our mothers' wombs. Every developmental stage we transition into involves the loss of the pleasant aspects of the one before. We lose youth, innocence, friends, relatives, money, pets, and on and on.

We begin teaching our children in the second year of life when to use the word "sad" to express the feelings accompanying loss. Ideally, we also teach them that when they feel mad about something they don't like, they might also be feeling sad about a loss. They learn much later in their development that prolonged sadness about a person or object that is seen as very important to them leads to a deeper and more painful form of sadness that we call sorrow.

Psychotherapists will tell you that the crazy-making sorrow that most of us have stored in our nonconscious is almost always the old emotion that has brought their patients into treatment. The human brain tends to equate deeply held and historically old sorrow with the fear of death. I'm sure that you have noticed that many people who are weeping from old sorrow almost can't breathe, exacerbating the fear that experiencing sorrow might kill you. But being able to fully experience sorrow is one of the most valuable parts of being human. It demonstrates that we have the ability to connect to others deeply—that we have the ability to attach such importance to others that being hurt by them or losing them makes us very sad.

Sorrow is a highly vulnerable emotion,[2] so it naturally follows that safety is essential to setting the stage for the conscious experience of sorrow. I have found that it is necessary for couples to go through many repairing dramas about their other unmetabolized emotions before their nonconscious storage bins can begin off-loading sorrow. Both partners need to know that their emotions will be handled with the utmost empathy, understanding, and care before they will risk feeling old sorrow together.

Katherine and John

Before this couple came for treatment, Katherine had been in her own individual therapy. So she already had some awareness of the sad feelings she had about her childhood and about how her family of origin had not met her needs. She had an autocratic father who did not allow for expressions of independent thought and action from anyone in the family. Katherine had taken him on by advocating for herself, in contrast to her mother, who had allowed herself to be completely dominated by her husband. Katherine had often pled with her mother to stand up for herself or get a divorce.

On the other hand, John had almost completely idealized his family, so he had no awareness of the sadness stored in his nonconscious storage bin about his childhood. He thought it was great that his parents had allowed for his freedom of expression by not being very strict. Unbeknownst to him, John had been forced into a role of being more of an adult than his parents when their marriage faltered. He denied that their divorce while he was in college had any negative effect on him, even though he could see how his younger brother had suffered.

You can see how their dramas of opposites had been set up by their experiences in their families. Katherine's father was autocratic; John's parents gave him almost no direction. Katherine's parents stayed together; John's parents divorced. This couple's nonconscious storage bins were both attempting *and* avoiding the experience of permanent loss and sorrow.

Figure 15.1. Katherine and John's recycling drama of opposites

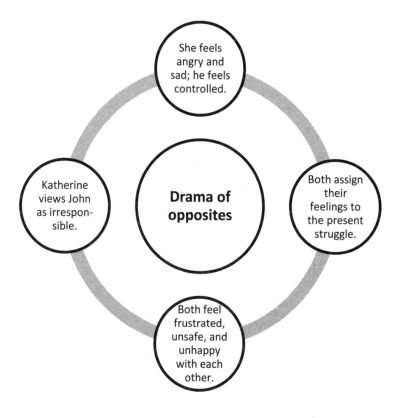

Rather than continuing to feel victimized in her marriage, Katherine told John how his disregard for her needs was a repetition of the way she had been and was still being treated by her family of origin. John was having much greater difficulty mourning the childhood he didn't have. Preparing for repairing dramas together set the stage for their brains to "accidentally" create a dialogue in which *both* of them could metabolize their sorrow.

Katherine: "How are you coming on that paper you have to do for your class?"

[*John's usual repetition of his parents' laissez-faire disciplining had caused him to not complete his college degree. He was trying to finish it so that he could pursue the career track he claimed to want.*]

John: "Stop pushing me about that paper. It's none of your business if I've finished it."

Katherine: "What do you mean it's none of my business? We're in this relationship together, and I care about how you're doing with your class."

John: "No, you don't. You just want to tell me what to do."

Katherine: [*beginning to cry*] "You know, this kind of reaction from you always makes me so sad. You don't know anything about what caring is. Your parents never cared enough to make you grow up. So here you are stuck with having to finish college now. And all those credit card debts you have—those are their fault, too."

John: "Now wait a minute. They were doing the best they could."

Katherine: "That's true, but you got hurt in the process. They were having marital problems, and your mother wanted to come to you as her 'friend' instead of being your mother. And now you feel obligated to take care of your father since their divorce, instead of being able to focus on taking care of yourself and us."

[*John pauses to stay safe and access his own feelings about his father. Katherine gives him plenty of time to feel his emotions.*]

John:　　　"He's such a sad, lonely man. I feel so sorry for him."

Katherine:　[*tolerating both her and John's sorrow*] "Yeah, and I don't want *you* to end up that way."

[*John pauses again. He's never thought of it this way.*]

Figure 15.2. Katherine and John's repairing drama

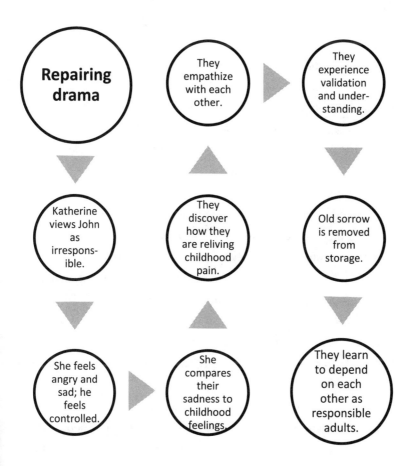

John: "Maybe you're right. It's his own fault that he's alone. He has never taken any responsibility for having the life he wants, and I get tired of doing everything for him."

Katherine: "Like I have to do for you?"

[*John feels stunned, but he doesn't react defensively. He allows his childhood pain to surface.*]

John: "I'm so sorry. I guess because I didn't want to see my parents as not caring I haven't been very caring toward you." [*taking responsibility*]

Katherine: "They were just too caught up in their own problems, like my parents. But we can do better for each other."

John: "That's what I want to do."

[*Their conversation ends with an embrace.*]

Karen and Bob

You have read in the previous chapter about all of the hard work that Karen and Bob did to metabolize other emotions in their nonconscious storage bins. The safety that was going to be necessary in order to experience repairing dramas about sorrow had been established in earlier dramas. Changing their relationship into a place of understanding and support prepared them to be able to successfully metabolize the massive losses from their childhoods that they both had to consciously feel.

The following conversation wasn't so much a repairing drama as it was simply an experience in metabolizing sorrow.

Karen: "You look really down today."

Bob: [*with tears rimming his eyelids*] "I'm just so sad about Eric [*their twenty-four-year-old son*] leaving."

Karen: "But he's left before."

Bob: "I know, but this time it feels like he's leaving for good." [*pausing and beginning to cry*] "I don't think he'll ever live with us again."

Karen: [*being curious*] "What about that is making you so much more sad than before?"

Bob: "I think it's the end of the dream." [*now sobbing*]

Karen: "The end of what dream?" [*wanting to know him better*]

Bob: "I've never said this before, but I had a 'dream' that having our happy family together would somehow cure the fact that I didn't have a happy family that stayed together."

[*Karen gives both of them time to feel his sorrow before saying . . .*]

Karen: "We've probably both thought that being happy together would change the past, but now we know that we can't do anything to change how bad our childhoods were."

Bob: "I know that I used the dream to chase away the sorrow I was always trying not to feel about what my mother did to our family. The hard work we've done to keep our family together has also made me realize all the anger and sadness I have about wondering why my father didn't try harder to stay in my life. He always said that he tried everything he could, but I think he was just intimidated by my mother."

Karen: "I know what you mean. All of us kids wanted to see our mother as an innocent and powerless victim of our dad. It has made me feel very sad to see her continue to stay with him through all these years, even though he's still so mean to her. She acts like she can't do anything about it, which is exactly why I always ended up feeling like I had to protect everyone at home from Dad. I'm so sorry that I saw you as being just like him to keep me away from the sorrow about my mother."

[*They pause quietly again.*]

Bob: "Thank you for hanging in there with me. I know I've made it hard sometimes."

Karen: "We both did our part of making it hard."

WHY ARE YOU DRIVING ME CRAZY?

Richard and Carol

There was a tremendous amount of unmetabolized loss and sorrow in the stories of Richard and Carol. Her mother had recently died of cancer, and his parents had divorced when he was a young adult. Carol was raised by a mother who had never recovered from the death of her first husband and a father who had effectively abandoned her by his rather quick remarriage after the death of her mother. Richard had continually experienced during his childhood the loss of being unconditionally loved by his family of origin. And this couple was reliving all of these losses by bringing painful sadness and sorrow into their marriage.

Carol: "I feel so sad about living apart."

Richard: "I just had to be on my own for a while."

Carol: "I know, but don't you feel sad too?"

Richard: "That's hard for me. I guess I just numb out instead of feeling sad. And when I think about the things my family did to me, I only feel angry. Maybe being sad feels too much like depression. I've always liked it better when you do all of the hard feelings for both of us." [*He chuckles quietly to himself.*]

Carol: "How well I know." [*She has a look that says she knows he's teasing her about the work they've done on taking responsibility for their own emotions.*]

[*With the playful teasing having created some safety for both of them, they pause to be with their own feelings for a moment.*]

Richard: "I can feel it when I think about your mother's death."

Carol: "Yeah, me too." [*another pause as a new revelation hits her*] "But I think that your leaving me also brought up sadness about my father leaving me."

Richard: "What do you mean your father leaving you?"

[*By this point in their work together, Carol and Richard had gotten very adept at using their repairing dramas to know each other and themselves better.*]

160

Carol: "That's the way it felt when he got remarried so soon after my mother's death. It's like he was just waiting for her to die. He couldn't be there for me in my sorrow, because he was all involved with his new wife. I can't relate to him anymore. They're both so religious; I feel left out." [*She cries.*]

Richard: "I know what you mean about not being able to relate to him. That's how it was with my family—they couldn't relate to me, and they didn't try. They just got upset when I tried to be my own person. They thought that they could even tell me how to dress when the family was going out somewhere. They didn't get me at all."

Carol: "I think you've wanted to tell yourself that I didn't get you at all. I think that's part of why you had to get away from me. So we had to leave each other, instead of feeling how sad it is that our families left *us*." [*mourning the end of childhood*]

Richard: "Really? You think that's what's been going on between us?"

Carol: "Sure feels like it to me."

Linking the sorrow of their marital problems to the sorrow of their childhood losses was the key to Richard's readiness to end the marital separation. When he knew that his fear and pain were not about the marriage, he could experience his desire to be with his wife, and he could be appreciatively moved by her patience with their repairing dramas. Carol came to know that the only way she could have become aware of the loss of her mother's love and her father's presence in her life was through the pain of almost losing her marriage.

Figure 15.3. Richard and Carol's repairing drama

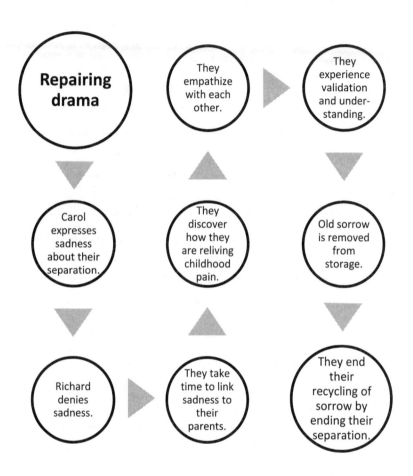

CHAPTER 16

Creating Permanent Growth

I have often used an analogy with my patients of thinking of psychological growth and development as a superhighway, with the exits representing developmental milestones. Typically, our parents will be capable of taking us only one "exit" further than they were able to go on the developmental "highway." Without specialized intervention, it is difficult for our parents to do much more than their parents could do to help their children developmentally. Usually, it's not that their intentions are limited, but it is impossible to develop capacities without the resources necessary to develop them. Our parents also have psychologies that were determined by *their* parents' limitations.

The experience of self in our relationship templates dictates that we will couple with a person whose psychological development is at about the same stage as our own—in other words, intimate partners have been dropped off at the same developmental "exit." While the behavioral manifestations of the stage in development will look quite different, partners are approximately the same developmental age in terms of the issues and tasks that have not been completed and that they are reliving together.[1]

The nonconscious matching of this element requires that one partner operate from the stage of development that is common to both partners, while the other looks like the more mature, parenting adult. For example, if your parents did not know how to help you successfully complete the adolescent stage of development, you will choose a mate who is in the same developmental predicament of being a partial child in an adult's body. One of you will behave like the teenage child, and the other will behave as an overadapted adult parent who *wishes* he or she could act as adolescent as the partner.

Being at the same stage of development would seem to foster an enjoyment and understanding of each other, and it does if that stage is adulthood. However, any developmental age that is less mature than adulthood requires a different structure for getting emotional dependency needs met than the marital relationship is designed to provide. Since most recycling dramas are an attempt to keep reliving childhood, both partners are nonconsciously expecting to be parented by their partner, and it will be close to impossible for them to negotiate a successful peer adult partnership.

It is appropriate for children and adolescents to blatantly and openly use their parents as objects for their developmental use. They should not have to see their parents' needs on par with their own. But partners must be able to see each other's needs as equally important to both of them. We must be able to simultaneously attend to our own needs and our partners' needs in order to be a successful mate. So if spouses are both still working on developmental issues at the younger than adult level, they will often have trouble meeting each other's needs as partners.

The goal of metabolizing the emotions that are part of our relationship templates is to release our brains from having to put energy into reliving the past and instead free new energy for getting on with our psychological growth and development,[2] from wherever our parents dropped us off. Human brains have a hierarchy for focusing attention and energy.

Perceived danger focuses brains on saving themselves. Brains must feel safe in order to grow; repairing dramas create an atmosphere of safety that is necessary in order to develop beyond the past.

When the process of safely and successfully emptying their nonconscious storage bins has been established, a couple will naturally get back on that "developmental highway." Since they were both dropped off at the same "exit" by their parents, getting back on that "highway" through repairing dramas will be experienced as natural and seamless. Proceeding further down the highway, both partners will spontaneously begin to show the capacity to take in aspects of the other that are helpful to their psychological growth and development, those aspects that they have probably been experiencing in dramas of opposites. They will learn from each other the parts of being human that the other already does well, leading to a more balanced and mature adult self in both partners. They will create a new *conscious* relationship between them where they can both safely explore the development of aspects of themselves that were previously unknown and even unimagined.[3]

You probably noticed some of these changes happening to our couples as you read the stories of their repairing dramas in the second part of this book. Let's take a look at the permanent growth toward a better developed and more fulfilled life that our couples created through their repairing dramas.

Bill and Sally

The crazy-making feelings of abandonment and loneliness that had been endlessly repeated in this marriage began to vanish. Bill and Sally learned that they could negotiate their time together and apart so that both of them could get what they needed and wanted. They made great strides in being able to listen to each other and provide emotional support without judgment or coercion. They began to experience the enjoyment of the differences between them in their strengths and weaknesses, which they used appropriately to help them get through important life transitions, such as the death of Bill's father and their only child's departure for college. Their old pattern of "every man for himself" gave way to a sustained appreciation for their partnership.

Katherine and John

Grappling with the deep sorrow that both of them had from their childhoods released Katherine and John to get on with building a strong new marriage. Developing genuine empathy and understanding through hearing about their childhood wounds created a mutual commitment to not continue wounding each other in the present. Through being able to see the fullness of each other—instead of the "half-baked" persons required by their recycling dramas—they began their marriage with the desire to help each other fulfill their adult dreams as true partners. After their wedding, John finished his degree and found a good job in another state. A few years later I received a letter with a picture of their two beautiful children. They told me of their continuing use of the work we had done together to construct the happy lives they now have.

Cynthia and Matthew

Learning to change their recycling dramas into repairing dramas freed Cynthia and Matthew from having to continually repeat their "good mother/bad child" pattern. Whenever it threatened to assert itself again during periods of life stress, it only took a small reminder to get them to relinquish the need to relive the old half-person view of each other. Then they could get back to supporting each other's growth and development.

Both Cynthia and Matthew made significant life changes through the process of repairing dramas. They had both gotten caught up in caretaking patterns with their families of origin which were destructive to their current family. They had been expending more energy on being concerned and trying to fix the problems of the families they grew up in than on their own family. Their repairing dramas included negotiating better boundaries that clearly placed the needs of their current family as priorities over their original families. They had new energy for each other and for parenting their own children as supportive partners.

Matthew was miserable in his career as a physician. He had simply followed in his father's footsteps without really exploring whether that was his own choice. Repairing dramas allowed him to depend on his relationship with Cynthia as a place where he could finally do that exploring about himself. Together they helped him to transition into a new career that was more about him. At the same time, they worked out a plan in which Cynthia could go back to graduate school and pursue her dreams as well.

Their repairing dramas also prepared them to deal with the major life transitions involved in their children growing into adults. Their brains were free to make constructive mutual decisions about how much to help and how much to set limits with their young adult children. Their old recycling dramas had created destructive patterns in their family that had historically allowed their children to come between them. These were replaced with the ability to work together as parents to make plans that were good for their children's development and that protected the health of their marriage. They learned that there was nothing hopeless about their marriage, and they became the greatest source of strength and encouragement for each other.

Karen and Bob

The amount of painful work that Karen and Bob put into saving their marriage was impressive and admirable. Having brought the hell of their childhoods into their marriage through domestic violence, the evolution their relationship accomplished is a tribute to their perseverance and courage in unearthing and exploring the excruciating emotions of childhood abuse and neglect. Transitioning their recycling dramas into repairing dramas meant struggling with relinquishing their roles as victim and villain and realizing that their mutual wishes to magically escape their pasts was only destroying their current relationship.

Their repairing dramas resulted in the blossoming of a truly loving and satisfying marriage for Bob and Karen. They became genuine supporters of each other as they grappled with changes in Bob's career and a crisis in his health. They got good at responding to Karen's family with appropriate levels of concern but also appropriate boundaries. They began to enjoy their hikes and games together, because there was no longer any need for recycling dramas. For about three years after they stopped treatment with me, I received holiday cards from them, telling me how well they were doing.

Brad and Carolyn

The immensity and intensity of the painful emotions that Brad and Carolyn endured in order to hold on to their marriage through major obstacles was remarkable. Many couples would have given up sooner, but they didn't want that, so they kept hanging in there through torturous repetitions of their childhood misery.

The key to their transformation was learning that instead of putting their energies into trying to "make" each other happy, they should create a safe place for both of them to express their childhood pain as much as they needed to metabolize those many old, crazy-making emotions from the past. Carolyn expressed toward the end of therapy that her old anger had completely disappeared. She was still working on the fear, shame, and sadness that are usually connected to feeling unworthy of love, but she was mostly aware that these emotions belonged to her childhood past.

Brad learned that Carolyn was not responsible for his feelings of inadequacy—his mother planted those seeds. This realization helped him to stay more calm when faced with Carolyn's disagreement or disappointment about something he had done. He became a much safer and emotionally dependable spouse, and he was a loving partner to Carolyn as she lived through a scary health crisis. All of this work on staying safe for metabolizing old emotions freed Brad and Carolyn to enjoy their retirement for the first time. The scars of the pain they inflicted on each other are still there, but they now know how they got there and what to do about them. They know that their improved marriage is a work in progress.

Charles and Kristine

It was quite a revelation to Charles and Kristine that their childhood experiences had taught them to feel ashamed for having normal human needs. And even more surprising to them was how compelled they both were to follow shame with suffering. The suffering continued after their wedding around Kristine's problems with her eyes and their mutual roles of putting others' needs before their enjoyment of their new marriage. They had barely returned from their honeymoon when Kristine felt obligated to stay with her family in another state to help with health issues of relatives for several weeks.

Learning that it is not shameful to have needs was the key to releasing Charles' and Kristine's energies toward enjoying their lives together. They became adept at catching the attempts of their nonconscious storage bins to inject suffering into their lives. They began to take responsibility for setting appropriate boundaries with relatives—and ex-relatives—as they constructed a relationship in which both of them could get their needs met. They can now always count on each other to talk through whatever issues and feelings come up between them, and they continue to use their dependable and safe connection to keep metabolizing old childhood emotions together.

The problems with Kristine's eyes have improved, and she is finally enjoying her retirement. Charles has also worked out an extended plan for his retirement with his employer, and he has gradually had much more time for traveling and fun activities with Kristine. They have used what they have learned about negotiating with each other, while allowing time to honor childhood feelings, to do some remodeling in their home, and come to some agreements about handling holiday times. Since their shame has been mostly healed, they have become free to negotiate a life together that doesn't allow suffering. They waited many years for the happiness they now share, and they want to relish every moment of the rest of their lives together.

Richard and Carol

Continuing to work on their marriage during a six-month separation proved to be the extensive repairing drama that set Richard and Carol on a new path of growth and development. They learned to negotiate a relationship with each other in which they felt equally powerful and equally regarded. Carol changed jobs, which gave her more time to pursue her passion for art. Shortly after they reconciled and moved back in together, she presented an exhibition of her paintings in a local art gallery. Simultaneously, Richard took full responsibility for deciding that he was OK with continuing the corporate job and doing his art on the side. He was fully supportive of Carol's show, and she used her contacts to help Richard sell some of his pieces.

During their repairing dramas, they began appropriately adult discussions about starting a family, as you read in chapter 14. As their needs to relive old crazy-making feelings gradually subsided, no one was pushing; no one was rushing; no one was running. Richard had an opportunity to fully explore his fearful feelings about becoming a parent, which had understandably arisen from his own bad experiences with being parented. Carol was quite empathic with his explorations of his old emotions, and Richard was clear that he knew how important it was for Carol to be a mother. When they stopped treatment with me, they had successfully negotiated the purchase of a new home that had adequate space for both of them, but they were still working on the family idea. It brought a smile to my lips when I received a picture of their new baby girl about a year after they finished couples therapy.

Jana and Rick

Healing the inadequacy and shame that were the legacy of our childhoods freed my husband and me to experience the blossoming of our talents in ways that we had never risked before. Pursuing the writing and publishing of this book would not have happened without the repairing dramas in my marriage. My husband has said that our many years of working on healing each other helped him develop the self-confidence to succeed in business. I have an avocational talent as a classical singer, and the best singing I ever did was created by the love and support I felt through our repairing dramas. Dancing the tango together in Buenos Aires on my sixtieth birthday was only one of hundreds of sweet rewards for accepting the challenge of transforming together.

Conclusion

Engaging in the steps toward transformation is an exercise in maturing. Developing patience, empathy, and genuine concern—as well as being on the receiving end of these new patterns of relating—creates caring grown-ups who have learned how to tolerate and process the full range of emotions that make us human. This process prepares people to live real life truly free of their old unfinished business and confident that together they can handle whatever is yet to come.[4]

Couples whose brain energies are released through repairing dramas will be able to pursue individual and joint dreams that they couldn't even see before.[5] Talents blossom; anxieties disappear; challenges are welcomed. Relationships free of the need for recycling dramas become sources of support and genuine love, based on the enjoyment of present lives that can now mutually plan for a fulfilling future.[6] Harnessing the constructive power of the dramas of marriage is the best route nature can provide us to changing for good.

APPENDIX A

The Science Behind *Why Are You Driving Me Crazy?*

M y study of four bodies of knowledge about the psychology of intimate relationships formed the theoretical foundations for the content of this book. By necessity I describe these four schools of thought below as separate and distinct entities, but there has been considerable overlap and interplay between these theory pioneers and expert practitioners. Their collective works have enhanced, built on, and confirmed each other's discoveries, giving us a coherent, consistent, and exciting new set of understandings about making sense of human behavior.

Following my brief description of each theory, I list the primary experts and researchers who developed the body of work in each area, along with their publications that I consulted in the process of writing *Why Are You Driving Me Crazy*. In addition, I also list the works of practitioners whose application of these theories informed my work. You will see most of these books and articles referenced in the "Notes" section below. However, if I do not specifically cite a work there, you should be aware that it nevertheless was an important source for this book.

The following list is not intended in any way to be inclusive of everything that has been written in these important areas of psychological inquiry. That would take an entire book itself. For example, I have often only included the first or most significant work of a particular theory pioneer or practitioner, or sometimes the most recent edition of an important book. My intent is to show you a sampling of the brilliant thinkers who have framed my professional work with couples.

1. Intersubjectivity—A Systems Theory

Intersubjectivity theory asserts that any two (or more) people within a relationship create a system of being together that is mutually influencing and unique to that relationship. It questions the notion that we all have an individual psychology that is determined by our genetics and childhood experiences and cannot be influenced by new relationships. Intersubjectivists believe that we are always responding to both the conscious and unconscious experiences of those in our relational field and being influenced by others in a profound way.

Theory pioneers of intersubjectivity theory—

Atwood, George E. & Stolorow, Robert D. (1993). *Faces in a Cloud: Intersubjectivity in Personality Theory.* Northvale, NJ: Jason Aronson.

Mitchell, Stephen A. (2000). *Relationality: From Attachment to Intersubjectivity.* Hillsdale, NJ: The Analytic Press.

Stolorow, Robert D.; Brandchaft, Bernard; & Atwood, George E. (1987). *Psychoanalytic Treatment: An Intersubjective Approach.* Hillsdale, NJ: The Analytic Press.

Stolorow, Robert D. & Atwood, George E. (1992). *Contexts of Being: The Intersubjective Foundations of Psychological Life.* Hillsdale, NJ: The Analytic Press.

Trevarthen, Colwyn. (1980). "The foundations of intersubjectivity: Development of interpersonal and co-operative understanding of infants." In David R. Olson, Ed., *The Social Foundations of Language and Thought* (pp. 316–342). New York: W.W. Norton & Company.

Practitioners of intersubjectivity theory—

Aron, Lewis. (1996). *A Meeting of Minds: Mutuality in Psychoanalysis.* Hillsdale, NJ: The Analytic Press.

Shaddock, David. (2000). *Contexts and Connections: An Intersubjective Systems Approach to Couples Therapy.* New York: Basic Books.

2. Attachment Theory and Infant Research

Attachment theory is composed of a huge body of knowledge that was spawned by the work of John Bowlby, a British psychoanalyst and academic, in the 1960s. His assistants, students, and protégés have contributed hundreds of research studies of the relationship between infants and their mothers to the professional literature on attachment theory. The development of the theory has focused on the biologically programmed responses and internal experiences of both babies and mothers in the critically important process of them becoming attached to each other at the beginning of a child's life. In addition, many disciples of attachment theory have explored its application to attachment styles evident in adult relationships.

Theory pioneers of attachment theory—

Ainsworth, Mary D. Salter; Blehar, Mary C.; Waters, Everett; & Wall, Sally. (1978). *Patterns of Attachment: A Psychological Study of the Strange Situation.* Hillsdale, NJ: Lawrence Erlbaum.

Bowlby, John. (1969). *Attachment and Loss. Vol. 1: Attachment.* New York: Basic Books.

----- (1973). *Attachment and Loss. Vol. 2: Separation, Anxiety and Anger.* New York: Basic Books.

----- (1981). *Attachment and Loss. Vol. 3: Loss, Sadness and Depression.* New York: Basic Books.

Main, Mary & Solomon, Judith. (1986). "Discovery of an insecure-disorganized/disoriented attachment pattern." In T. Berry Brazelton & Michael W. Yogman (Eds.), *Affective Development in Infancy.* Norwood, NJ: Ablex.

Stern, Daniel N. (1977). *The First Relationship: Infant and Mother.* Cambridge, Massachusetts: Harvard University Press.

----- (1985). *The Interpersonal World of the Infant: A View from Psychoanalysis and Developmental Psychology.* New York: Basic Books.

Practitioners of attachment theory—
Beebe, Beatrice, & Lachmann, Frank M. (2002). *Infant Research and Adult Treatment: Co-constructing Interactions.* Hillsdale, NJ: Analytic Press.

Brazelton, T. Berry, M.D., & Cramer, Bertrand G., M.D. (1990). *The Earliest Relationship: Parents, Infants, and the Drama of Early Attachment.* Reading, Massachusetts: Addison-Wesley Publishing Company.

Karen, Robert. (1994). *Becoming Attached: Unfolding the Mystery of the Infant-Mother Bond and Its Impact on Later Life.* New York: Warner Books.

3. Neuroscience
The research of neuroscientists proliferated in the 1980–90s as new technologies made it possible to directly study the human brain in ways that had never been possible before. Their work began to document and prove that almost all of the discoveries of psychology theorists in the past

could be physically observed and are therefore biologically programmed into our brains. Neuroscientists expanded the utility of the first two groups of theory described above by confirming them through scientific study of the brain.

One of the interesting facts about the development of neuroscience as a professional discipline is that it was primarily inspired by wanting to understand what is happening to the human brain when things go wrong. Interest in psychological trauma often spurred the first studies that brought neuroscience into the forefront of inquiry into human nature.

Theory pioneers in neuroscience—

Fosha, Diana; Siegel, Daniel J.; & Solomon, Marion F., Eds. (2009). *The Healing Power of Emotion: Affective Neuroscience, Development, and Clinical Practice.* New York: W.W. Norton & Company—Chapters 1 through 6.

Gallese, Vittorio. (2009). "Mirror neurons, embodied simulation, and the neural basis of social identification." *Psychoanalytic Dialogues,* Vol. 19, pp. 519–536.

Panksepp, Jaak. (1998). *Affective Neuroscience: The Foundations of Human and Animal Emotions.* New York: Oxford University Press.

Schore, Allan N. (1994). *Affect Regulation and the Origin of the Self: The Neurobiology of Emotional Development.* Hillsdale, NJ: Lawrence Erlbaum Associates.

Siegel, Daniel J. (2012). *The Developing Mind: How Relationships and the Brain Interact to Shape Who We Are,* 2nd ed. New York: The Guilford Press.

Practitioners of neuroscience—

Cozolino, Louis. (2006). *The Neuroscience of Human Relationships: Attachment and the Developing Social Brain.* New York: W.W. Norton.

4. Affective Therapies

As neuroscientific research progressed, mounting evidence suggested that the part of the human brain that contains our emotions (affects)—the right hemisphere of the brain—is where therapeutic action has to take place in order to address people's psychological and relationship issues. Thus, affective therapies that help patients access, regulate, and process their emotions emerged. This trend questioned the efficacy of cognitive/ behavioral (left-brain) techniques that had proliferated from the 1960s through the 1980s as a backlash to the focus on the unconscious taught in the psychodynamic tradition.

Right-brain therapies primarily focus on the regulation of disrupted and disruptive emotional states that are interfering with patients' abilities to function well in life. Examples of affective therapies are Diana Fosha's Accelerated Experiential-Dynamic Psychotherapy (AEDP) and Susan Johnson's Emotionally Focused Therapy (EFT) with couples.

Theory pioneers of affective therapies—

Fosha, Diana; Siegel, Daniel J.; & Solomon, Marion F., Eds. (2009). *The Healing Power of Emotion: Affective Neuroscience, Development, and Clinical Practice.* New York: W.W. Norton & Company—Chapters 7 through 11.

Practitioners of affective therapies—

Fosha, Diana. (2000). *The Transforming Power of Affect: A Model For Accelerated Change.* New York: Basic Books.

APPENDIX A

Greenberg, Leslie S. & Goldman, Rhonda N. (2008). *Emotion-Focused Couples Therapy: The Dynamics of Emotion, Love, and Power.* Washington, DC: American Psychological Association.

Johnson, Susan M. (2004). *The Practice of Emotionally Focused Couples Therapy: Creating Connection* (2nd ed.). New York: Brunner-Routledge.

Solomon, Marion & Tatkin, Stan. (2011). *Love and War in Intimate Relationships: Connection, Disconnection, and Mutual Regulation in Couple Therapy.* New York: W.W. Norton & Company.

Wile, Daniel B. (1993). *Couples Therapy: A Nontraditional Approach.* New York: John Wiley & Sons.

APPENDIX B

Exercises for Applying *Why Are You Driving Me Crazy?* to Your Relationship

To assist you in using this book to improve your own relationship, I have provided here some questions and activities for applying what you have read to yourself and your partner. You might find it useful to write down your responses, but certainly you and your partner should discuss together what you are discovering about yourselves and your relationship.

Chapter 1 – Characteristics of the Dramas of Marriage

1. Write down a repetitive "script" that you and your partner find yourselves caught up in regularly. It will be a dialogue in which you both end up feeling bad the same way every time, and you both have some sense that you know what each of you is going to say again. If you think of more than one script, write them all down.

2. See if you and your partner can identify the bad feelings that you usually have at the end of your particular dramas. This will help both of you pinpoint what your own unmetabolized emotions are.

3. Which roles are you and your partner likely to play in your repetitive dramas? Is one of you the "child" and one of you the "parent"? Is one of you "always right" and the other "always wrong"? Is one of you begging and the other always saying "no"? Is one of you aggressive and the other passive? There are many, many ways that partners experience reciprocal roles in marital dramas. See if you can figure out what yours are.

Chapter 2 – The Brain as Casting Director

1. Using the information that you and your partner discovered as you identified your reciprocal roles in your marital dramas, draw your matching relationship template. Think about how the ways you experience yourselves and yourselves with others get played out in your marital dramas.

2. Which of the emotions shown in Figure 2.2 are you and your partner both feeling during your marital dramas? These will probably be the emotions that you identified during your chapter 1 exercise #2. Remember, your crazy-making feelings are the same, even if only one of you seems to be consciously feeling them during your dramas.

Chapter 3 – Dramas of Opposites

1. Have you tried to avoid your crazy-making feelings by becoming a half-person in your intimate relationship? Are you experiencing all of the emotions that really belong to both you and your partner, or have you both nonconsciously "agreed" that one of you will do some feelings and the other one different feelings?

2. See if you can identify the emotions that you might be avoiding by acting like they are coming only from your partner.

Chapter 4 – Competition Dramas

1. Do you and your partner get into arguments about which one of you is right?
2. Do you and your partner try to prove which one of you is the better person?
3. Do your marital dramas include looking for some kind of proof that one or both of you deserve to get what you need?
4. Do you argue over who is entitled to their feelings, based on behavior in the marriage?

Chapter 5 – Victims and Villains Dramas

1. Does one of you primarily get characterized as the villain and the other primarily feel victimized in your marital dramas? Or do the two of you switch these roles in different dramas?
2. Can you identify who the "victims" and "villains" were in your family of origin?

Chapter 6 – Shame/Reunion Dramas

1. What do you do in your marriage that makes you feel inadequate or ashamed? Or what does your partner tell you that you do that *should* make you feel inadequate or ashamed?
2. If you are feeling inadequate or ashamed in your intimate relationship, what do you do to get back into your partner's "good graces"?
3. Does your partner shame you, or do you shame your partner?
4. Is only one of you identified as the "bad" person in your marriage? Does that person express any shame for his/her behavior?

Chapter 7 – Turning Recycling Dramas into Repairing Dramas

1. Use all of the information that you have discovered above to draw diagrams of your recycling dramas. You might want to refer

to the examples of recycling dramas in this and later chapters to help you draw your own dramas.

2. Filling out the diagrams of your recycling dramas will help you get clearer about the specific crazy-making feelings that you and your partner are reliving.

3. Keep in mind that recycling dramas are circular, meaning that they will end right where they started. You will both feel bad the same way at the end as at the beginning.

Chapter 8 – Assuring Safety

1. Do you and your partner feel safe with each other—physically, emotionally, mentally, sexually? If you are not physically safe in your relationship, you must take action right away to seek help for maintaining your physical safety.

2. If you do not feel safe, focus on what *you* can do to increase the safety of your relationship in the following areas:

   • Maintaining desire and commitment—

     If you aren't sure about staying in your marriage, you must take responsibility for making a clear decision about staying or leaving before you can move on. Hanging onto ambivalence about your marriage is probably a hiding place for important crazy-making feelings in your nonconscious storage bin that need to be metabolized.

     Make a permanent commitment by getting married (or some equivalent of marriage).

     Don't ever threaten to leave or get a divorce.

     Get out of that "other" relationship that you have imagined is perfect.

     Be aware of how you express your own feelings of desire toward your partner.

- Treating each other with respect—
  Treat your partner with the same regard that you want paid to you.
  Never use abusive language or character assassinations directed at your partner.
- Refusing the victim or villain role—
  If you think that you are truly being mistreated by your partner, take respectful and adult steps to make it stop.
  Never accept all the blame for a recycling drama or assume that your partner should.
  Do not succumb to believing that you are simply a bad person with unchangeable bad behavior.

Chapter 9 – Taking Responsibility

1. Before you and your partner can move on to repairing dramas, you must both believe that you are equally responsible for all the good parts and all the painful parts of your relationship.
2. Using the chart in Figure 9.1, identify the ways that you are putting these rules into practice in your intimate relationship.
3. Use the behaviors outlined in this chapter to again help you identify the crazy-making feelings that are waiting to be metabolized by you and your partner.

Chapter 10 – Tolerating Pain

1. What are the painful experiences from your childhoods that you thought you wouldn't have to deal with anymore as adults?
2. How have you and your partner been avoiding that pain?

Chapters 11 through 16

Now you are ready for repairing dramas. Use the diagrams of repairing dramas in the book in whichever ways would be most useful to you and your partner for metabolizing emotions from the past and moving on to the creation of permanent growth that you have hoped for within your own intimate relationship.

ACKNOWLEDGMENTS

I want to start my thank yous with the people that many authors leave for the end—my family. They are the ones who had to live with me during the long gestation of this book, and I will be eternally grateful to them for their patience and encouragement. My husband, Rick Poppe, not only tolerated many hours, days, and months of my concentration on something other than him; he also lived through the application of the contents of this work to our personal lives and courageously allowed me to share some of our challenging intimate moments with my readers. I think he would agree that the two of us changed each other for good; I thank him for taking many emotional risks with me.

My stepdaughter, Jennifer Poppe, JD, assisted me with some of the legal issues involved in this project, as well as reading many versions of the manuscript. My sister-in-law and brother-in-law, Bari and John Edstrom, contributed valuable feedback on the final draft, and my daughter-in-law, Lisa Sveland, provided continuous encouragement and support throughout the process of moving this book toward publication. Thank you all for being so loving and generous with your time.

The second most important group to thank is my patients. As stated in the introduction, I am particularly grateful to those couples who agreed to allow me to share their stories. I admire their courage and generosity in opening up their personal lives for the benefit of others. All good psychotherapists are continually aware of the privilege we experience every day in our offices that is granted to us by those people who come to us for help. It is an awesome responsibility and a special gift given to us by our patients to be invited into their vulnerabilities as part of the process of change. I want all of my patients to know how much I appreciate being given the opportunity to both help them and learn from them at the same time.

Now to the world of the many professionals who have contributed to my growth and development as a clinician. Two supervisors who stand out as particularly transformative were Ellenjean Morris, LCSW, and Dr. Michael Solomon, LCSW. Both of these clinical social workers pushed me beyond my previous limits and challenged me to think in new, dynamic ways. I thank them for not letting me "rest on my laurels" of past achievements. Additionally, the colleagues with whom I have shared a long-lived and highly valuable peer consultation group have taken risks together in service of developing each other's professional thinking. Thank you to Ina Mae Denham, LCSW, Katharine Rasé, LCSW, and Patricia Higgins, LCSW.

Others have graciously shared their time and professional knowledge in the process of my learning to translate my experiences as a clinician into the written word. Particular thanks go to a couple of mentors who encouraged my development as a writer: Lewis Aron, PhD, and Michael Nichols, PhD. Dr. Nichols generously helped me every step along the way in the development of this book. I also owe a debt of gratitude to the colleagues and friends who reviewed the many revisions of my manuscript and offered valuable advice: Jennifer Bess, LCSW; Dawn Sokolski, PhD; Bill Schneider, PhD; Kristine Schneider, MSW; Stacey Freedenthal, PhD, LCSW; Holly Adamek; and Deborah Barber. Many others consistently asked about my progress along the way, and I greatly appreciate all of their confidence demonstrated by encouraging me to continue the pursuit of my dream.

ACKNOWLEDGMENTS

The final group of people I want to thank are the professional editors whose talents have made me look like a decent writer. Kate Ankofski, Editorial Director at Langdon Street Press, knew all of the right changes I needed to incorporate to turn my manuscript into an appealing book, and Pam Nordberg went through the tedious and careful process that was necessary to ensure that each little detail was done properly. The last and most important player in this endeavor was the independent editor who showed me how to turn an OK group of ideas into a real book that people might actually want to read. I am immensely grateful to Chris Benton for generously giving of her professional expertise and time to help me clearly communicate to others what has been in my head for such a long time.

NOTES

Introduction

[1]   I have chosen to use the word *marriage* throughout this book because it is the term most widely used to describe a legally committed couple. However, all of the concepts in the book can be equally applied to any long-term committed couple for whom legal marriage is currently not an option.

[2]   Cozolino, Louis. (2006). *The Neuroscience of Human Relationships: Attachment and the Developing Social Brain.* New York: W.W. Norton & Company, p. 28.

Lewis, Michael; Haviland-Jones, Jeannette M.; & Barrett, Lisa Feldman, Eds. (2010). *Handbook of Emotions*, 3rd Ed. New York: The Guilford Press.

Siegel, Daniel J. (2012). *The Developing Mind: How Relationships and the Brain Interact to Shape Who We Are*, 2nd Ed. New York: The Guilford Press, pp. 193–194.

[3]   Solomon, Marion & Tatkin, Stan. (2011). *Love and War in Intimate Relationships: Connection, Disconnection, and Mutual Regulation in Couple Therapy.* New York: W.W. Norton & Company, pp. 215–231.

⁴   "(W)e may conclude that during periods of intense stress the brain's ability to form conscious memories is impaired, but its ability to form unconscious emotional memories is potentiated" (pp. 166–167). From Joseph E. Ledoux & Elizabeth A. Phelps (2010), "Emotional networks in the brain" (pp. 159–179), in Lewis, Haviland-Jones, & Barrett, Eds. (2010).

"Without painful feelings, all humans would die prematurely" (p. 59). From Jaak Panksepp (2010), "The affective brain and core consciousness: How does neural activity generate emotional feelings?" (pp. 47–67), in Lewis, Haviland-Jones, & Barrett, Eds. (2010).

"(I)t is now clear that humans store unconscious memories and unconsciously activate subcortical emotion centers of the brain" (p. 43). From Jan E. Stets & Jonathan H. Turner (2010), "The sociology of emotions" (pp. 32–46), in Lewis, Haviland-Jones, & Barrett, Eds. (2010).

⁵   Schore, Allan N. (1994). *Affect Regulation and The Origin of the Self: The Neurobiology of Emotional Development.* Hillsdale, New Jersey: Erlbaum.

Siegel (2012).

Solomon & Tatkin (2011), pp. 98–116.

⁶   Cozolino (2006).

Fosha, Diana; Siegel, Daniel J.; & Solomon, Marion F., Eds. (2009). *The Healing Power of Emotion: Affective Neuroscience, Development, and Clinical Practice.* New York: W.W. Norton & Company.

"(A)ttachment style is related to children's subsequent emotion regulation . . ." (p. 337). From Carolyn Saarni (2010), "The interface of emotional development with social context" (pp. 332–347), in Lewis, Haviland-Jones, & Barrett, Eds. (2010).

"(A)ttachment interactions are all about how dyadic regulation shapes self-regulation. In other words, the child learns to regulate her own states of arousal and inner processing through interactions with another" (p. 103). From Siegel (2012).

7   The use of the term *nonconscious* to describe the information that our brains store outside conscious awareness is becoming more widely used in the brain research literature than the term *unconscious*. This seems to avoid confusion with the medical use of the word unconscious, meaning literal loss of consciousness. I have found through the years that my patients spontaneously use the word *subconscious* to substitute for my word unconscious in an effort to avoid their own confusion. So I find the use of the term nonconscious to be less confusing and more scientifically accurate.

Some psychology theorists reserve the term unconscious for stimuli that have first been conscious and then repressed. There is mounting evidence that most of what we would consider unconscious material was never conscious in the first place. Again, the word nonconscious seems to convey this more clearly.

8   Cozolino (2006).

Fosha, Siegel, & Solomon, Eds. (2009).

Schore (1994).

Shaddock, David. (2005). *From Impasse to Intimacy: How Understanding Unconscious Needs Can Transform Relationships*. Lanham, Maryland: Jason Aronson, pp. 34–36.

Siegel (2012).

Solomon & Tatkin (2011).

9   Cozolino (2006), pp. 59 and 186–198.

Mirror neurons are "(n)erve cells that activate in sympathy and in the same brain location as the nerve cells of the person whose actions we are watching. This seems to be the physiological basis of imitation, our ability to participate in another's actions. These neurons help us sense what others intend and help us connect with what the other feels" (p. 274). From Dr. Sue Johnson (2008), *Hold Me Tight: Seven Conversations for a Lifetime of Love*. New York: Little, Brown and Company.

Larsen, Jeff T.; Berntson, Gary G.; Poehlmann, Kirsten M.; Ito, Tiffany A.; & Cacioppo, John T. (2010). "The psychophysiology of emotion" (pp. 180–195), in Lewis, Haviland-Jones, & Barrett, Eds. (2010).

Siegel (2012), pp. 164–166.

Walker-Andrews, Arlene S. (2010). "Intermodal emotional processes in infancy" (pp. 364–375), in Lewis, Haviland-Jones, & Barrett, Eds. (2010).

[10]   "We do not know how the physical property of neurons firing and the subjective experience of our inner mental lives mutually create each other" (p. 35). From Siegel (2012).

[11]   Several neurobiologically-oriented authors have written about unmetabolized emotions:

Shapiro, Francine & Laliotis, Deany (2011). "EMDR and the adaptive information processing model: Integrative treatment and case conceptualization" (pp. 191–200), *Clinical Social Work Journal*, Vol. 39, No. 2.

"(P)ockets of unmetabolized, painful experience can emerge under stress and increase instances of dysregulation" (p. 106). From Solomon & Tatkin (2011).

[12]   Stein, Ruth. (1999). *Psychoanalytic Theories of Affect*. London: Karnac Books.

NOTES

[13]   In Diana Fosha's chapter in Fosha, Siegel, & Solomon, Eds. (2009), entitled "Emotion and recognition at work: Energy, vitality, pleasure, truth, desire & the emergent phenomenology of transformational experience" (pp. 172–203), she describes this type of "healing as a biologically wired-in process" (p. 180). "Innate dispositional tendencies toward growth, learning, healing, and self-righting are wired deep within our brains and press toward expression when circumstances are right" (p. 174).

[14]   "(W)e must use words to attempt to understand the nature of emotion and the human mind . . . Studies have . . . shown that . . . [one] can 'name it to tame it'" (pp. 180–181). From Siegel (2012).

     Tronick, Ed. (2009). "Multilevel meaning making and dyadic expansion of consciousness theory: The emotional and the polymorphic polysemic flow of meaning" (pp. 86–111), in Fosha, Siegel, & Solomon, Eds. (2009).

[15]   "Language, in combination with emotional attunement, creates the opportunity to support neural growth and network integration" (p. 232). From Cozolino (2006).

     "(O)ld feelings can be integrated into new cognitive structures" (p. 26). From Jaak Panksepp (2009), "Brain emotional systems and qualities of mental life: From animal models of affect to implications for psychotherapeutics" (pp. 1–26), in Fosha, Siegel, & Solomon, Eds. (2009).

     In all of his work, Daniel Siegel (2009, "Emotion as integration: A possible answer to the question, what is emotion?" in Fosha, Siegel, & Solomon, Eds., pp. 145–171) and (2012) emphasizes the goal of integration as essential to mental health.

[16]   "This process of verbalization allows *previously unsymbolized* [alternatively, *unmetabolized*] experience in emotion memory to be

assimilated into people's conscious, conceptual understandings of self and world, where it can be organized into a coherent story" (p. 93). From Leslie S. Greenberg (2010), "The clinical application of emotion in psychotherapy" (pp. 88–101), in Lewis, Haviland-Jones, & Barrett, Eds. (2010).

"(T)he naming and repairing of emotional injuries is so important in self-development . . ." (p. 34). From Shaddock (2005).

"The experience of expressing one's emotional state and having others perceive and respond to those signals appears to be of vital importance in the development of the brain" (p. 155). From Siegel (2012).

[17]   Greenberg, Leslie S. & Goldman, Rhonda N. (2008). *Emotion-Focused Couples Therapy: The Dynamics of Emotion, Love, and Power.* Washington, DC: American Psychological Association.

Johnson, Susan M. (2004). *The Practice of Emotionally Focused Couples Therapy: Creating Connection,* 2nd Ed. New York: Brunner-Routledge.

Karen, Robert. (1994). *Becoming Attached: Unfolding the Mystery of the Infant-Mother Bond and Its Impact on Later Life.* New York: Warner Books.

Solomon & Tatkin (2011).

Sperling, Michael B. & Berman, William H., Eds. (1994). *Attachment in Adults: Clinical and Developmental Perspectives.* New York: The Guilford Press.

[18]   Gallese, Vittorio. (2009). "Mirror neurons, embodied simulation, and the neural basis of social identification," *Psychoanalytic Dialogues,* Vol. 19, pp. 519–536.

[19]   Hendrix, Harville, Ph.D. (1990). *Getting the Love You Want: A Guide for Couples.* New York: HarperPerennial.

NOTES

[20]   The psychological concept of the "repetition compulsion" was initially studied and described by Sigmund Freud (*The Standard Edition of the Complete Psychological Works of Sigmund Freud*, translated from the German under the general editorship of James Strachey, London: The Hogarth Press, 1958, Vol. 18). Conventional wisdom in the past was that, although the compulsion to repeat the past was universally seen in humans, it was considered unfortunate, pathological, and a problem to overcome. Robert Karen (1994) states, "We see Freud's 'repetition compulsion' in people who seek the same sort of partners again and again, exhibiting behavior that remains disturbingly consistent across relationships" (p. 395). My assertion here is that nonconscious repetitions of the past are a natural and necessary healing process of the human brain.

[21]   "True, partners are sometimes chosen who will repeat hurtfulness, but also, people choose partners who will offer the possibility of rehabilitation" (p. 7). From Mary-Joan Gerson (2010), *The Embedded Self: An Integrative Psychodynamic and Systemic Perspective on Couples and Family Therapy*, 2nd Ed. New York: Routledge.

[22]   "People who stay married live four years longer than people who don't" (p. 5); and "(W)orking briefly on your marriage every day will do more for your health and longevity than working out at a health club" (p. 261). From John M. Gottman, Ph.D. & Nan Silver (2000), *The Seven Principles for Making Marriage Work*. New York: Three Rivers Press.
        Johnson (2008), p. 24.

[23]   "Through the dyadic process, individuals often are able to emotionally process what they are not able to process alone" (p. 43). From Greenberg & Goldman (2008).

Chapter 1

[1]   Gerson (2010).

Johnson, Susan M. & Denton, Wayne. (2002). "Emotionally focused couple therapy: Creating secure connections" (pp. 221–250). In Alan S. Gurman & Neil S. Jacobson, Eds. (2002), *Clinical Handbook of Couple Therapy*, 3rd Ed. New York: The Guilford Press.

Johnson (2008).

Shaddock (2005).

Siegel (2012).

Solomon & Tatkin (2011).

[2]   "The relationship recreates a familiar pattern: our partner becomes our parent, and we react as we did as children" (p. 53). From Shaddock (2005).

"We recreate, in our intimate bonds, patterns of interaction that were scripted in our relationships with our primary caregiver(s), whether good or bad. These interactional patterns, once wired into the brain, tend to recreate themselves in each subsequent relationship throughout life" (p. 3). From Solomon & Tatkin (2011).

[3]   Gerson (2010).

Schore, Allan N. (2009). "Right-brain affect regulation: An essential mechanism of development, trauma, dissociation, and psychotherapy" (pp. 112–144), in Fosha, Siegel, & Solomon, Eds. (2009).

Siegel (2012).

[4]   "(E)motions must be 'up and running' and must be experienced for beneficial emotional processing to occur" (p. 92). From Greenberg (2010) in Lewis, Haviland-Jones, & Barrett, Eds. (2010).

NOTES

"What appears to be pathological enactment may be an attempt to share with another person emotions that are too primitive for words" (p. 237). From Marion Solomon (2009), "Emotion in romantic partners: Intimacy found, intimacy lost, intimacy reclaimed" (pp. 232–256), in Fosha, Siegel, & Solomon, Eds. (2009).

5   "Each partner has slowly taken on a role in the relationship that is familiar from early history and advanced by the history of interactions between them" (p. 253). From Solomon (2009) in Fosha, Siegel, & Solomon, Eds. (2009).

6   Jurkovic, Gregory J. (1997). *Lost Childhoods: The Plight of the Parentified Child.* Philadelphia, PA: Brunner/Mazel.

Gerson (2010), pp. 114 and 173.

Chapter 2

1   Brazelton, T. Berry, M.D., & Cramer, Bertrand G., M.D. (1990). *The Earliest Relationship: Parents, Infants, and the Drama of Early Attachment.* Reading, MA: Addison-Wesley Publishing Company.

Cozolino (2006).

Karen (1994).

Klaus, Marshall H., M.D., & Klaus, Phyllis H., M.Ed., C.S.W. (1985). *The Amazing Newborn.* Reading, MA: Addison-Wesley Publishing Company.

Stern, Daniel N. (1997). *The First Relationship: Infant and Mother.* Cambridge, MA: Harvard University Press.

2   Eliot, Lise, Ph.D. (1999). *What's Going on in There? How the Brain and Mind Develop in the First Five Years of Life.* New York: Bantam Books.

3   Dayton, Tian, Ph.D. (1997). *Heartwounds: The Impact of Unresolved Trauma and Grief on Relationships.* Deerfield Beach, Florida: Health Communications.

Terr, Lenore. (1990). *Too Scared to Cry: Psychic Trauma in Childhood.* New York: Basic Books.

4   Curtis, Rebecca C., Ed. (1991). *The Relational Self: Theoretical Convergences in Psychoanalysis and Social Psychology.* New York: The Guilford Press.

Stern, Daniel N. (1985). *The Interpersonal World of the Infant: A View from Psychoanalysis and Developmental Psychology.* New York: Basic Books.

5   "The internal working model [of attachment] . . . reflects the child's relationship history . . . , defining how he will feel about himself when he is closely involved with another person" (p. 209). From Karen (1994).

6   "(O)ne's understanding and experience of oneself is inextricably linked to one's experience of systemic others" (p. 23). From Gerson (2010).

7   In *Too Close for Comfort: Exploring the Risks of Intimacy* (New York: Plenum Press, Insight Books), clinical psychologist Geraldine Piorkowski, Ph.D., (1994) writes an entire book about the dangers of closeness. "As with the basic emotional needs, the particular fears that an individual experiences and their intensity are determined by both past and current relationships" (p. 16).

8   Dr. Piorkowski's (1994) list of the risks of closeness includes "vulnerability and shamefulness . . . [Fear] of losing control or losing

NOTES

autonomy . . . (F)earful of being attacked, disappointed, betrayed, or rejected . . . (F)earful about feeling overly responsible and guilty for all of the relationship's problems" (p. 16).

9   "[There is] increasingly solid evidence that children who are given opportunities to engage in family conversation about emotion end up with a more accurate and comprehensive understanding" (p. 320). From Paul L. Harris (2010), "Children's understanding of emotion" (pp. 320–331), in Lewis, Haviland-Jones, & Barrett, Eds. (2010).

"(P)articular emotional responses are commonly favored over others even in the best of families. The habitual interpretation of emotional arousal in predictable ways leads to biases toward certain emotions" (p. 219). From Pat Ogden (2009), "Emotion, mindfulness, and movement: Expanding the regulatory boundaries of the window of affect tolerance" (pp. 204–231), in Fosha, Siegel, & Solomon, Eds. (2009).

10   "The sounds, feel, and sight of the mother's expressive face elevate dopamine and endorphin levels, making the mother the infant's primary source of enjoyment and well-being . . . [and resulting in] heightened activity, excitement, and elation" (p. 101). From Cozolino (2006).

In *Intimate Partners: Patterns in Love and Marriage* (New York: Ballantine Books), author Maggie Scarf (1988) labels this experience "The Golden Fantasy: . . . the infant's wish to be merged, in a state of well-being and closeness, to the caregiving other . . ." She then describes the longing connected to this fantasy: "What will remain, somewhere deep within, will be a dimly perceived yearning for that time of total union, that Garden of Eden almost beyond remembering . . ." (p. 82).

11   For discussions of categories of emotions, see:
Lewis, Haviland-Jones, & Barrett, Eds. (2010); and Panksepp (2009) in Fosha, Siegel, & Solomon, Eds. (2009).

[12]   Herman, Judith. (1992). *Trauma and Recovery*. New York: Basic Books.

van der Kolk, Bessel A.; McFarlane, Alexander C.; & Weisaeth, Lars, Eds. (1996). *Traumatic Stress: The Effects of Overwhelming Experience on Mind, Body, and Society*. New York: The Guilford Press.

[13]   "(E)arly relational trauma, reactivated in . . . enactments, manifests in . . . panic/terror, rage, and pain . . . , as well as . . . shame, disgust, and hopeless despair . . ." (p. 130). From Schore (2009) in Fosha, Siegel, & Solomon, Eds. (2009).

[14]   "(W)hen two people fall in love, the seeds of their later conflicts are already present. Both carry their personal history wired into their brains, and these neural networks are waiting to be activated . . ." (p. 5). From Solomon & Tatkin (2011).

[15]   In Fosha, Siegel, & Solomon, Eds. (2009), Diana Fosha (2009) calls this "the felt sense of *feeling recognized* . . ." (p. 178) and Allan Schore (2009) states, "(O)ne unconscious mind communicates with another unconscious mind . . ." (p. 115).

"(T)he mirror properties in our brains enable us to imagine empathically what is going on inside another person" (pp. 165). From Siegel (2012).

[16]   In his chapter entitled "Collaborative Couple Therapy" (pp. 281–307), in Gurman & Jacobson, Eds. (2002), Daniel B. Wile (2002) labels this phenomenon in couples' relationships their "interacting sensitivities." "Each reacts to having his/her childhood-based special sensitivity stimulated in a way that stimulates that of the other" (p. 290).

NOTES

Chapter 3

[1] The major premise of Stephen A. Mitchell's (2002) book, *Can Love Last? The Fate of Romance Over Time* (New York: W.W. Norton & Company) is that the very act of transitioning from romance to marriage (or any of its equivalents) creates a dialectic between opposing psychological forces whose tension must be dealt with, and even enjoyed, throughout the life of the relationship. "Opposites attract because they are inversions of each other, the same thing in different forms . . . What is alluring in the other may not be the otherness of the other as much as the opportunity for making contact, at a safe distance, with disclaimed aspects of the self" (pp. 81–82).

Stan Tatkin (2011) uses the term "biphasic couples" to describe this phenomenon. From Solomon & Tatkin (2011), p. 101.

[2] "How tempting is it to divest oneself of an intolerable quality by cloning it on an intimate partner?" (p. 4). From Gerson (2010).

"(B)y fighting the battle out with the spouse, one does not have to experience it as what it is: a painful internal conflict which is actually taking place within one's own psyche" (p. 201). From Scarf (1988).

[3] "The mechanism of complementarity enables us to find in our mate parts of ourselves that we have repressed or denied through fear or disapproval but that we are eagerly seeking to express" (p. 100). From Judith S. Wallerstein & Sandra Blakeslee (1996), *The Good Marriage: How & Why Love Lasts* (New York: Warner Books).

[4] "(E)ach of us is drawn toward another who freely gives voice to what we also want but are afraid to let ourselves know about or express" (p. 38). From Mitchell (2002).

"We humans often try to get our mates to act out our disavowed, repudiated, dissociated feelings . . ." (p. 195). From Scarf (1988).

Shaddock (2005), p. 63.

[5]   "(T)hey have unwittingly chosen someone who manifests the very parts of their being that were cut off in childhood . . ." (p. 52). From Hendrix (1990).

Solomon & Tatkin (2011), p. 101.

Chapter 5

[1]   "Because we believe we are only reacting to our partners' provocations, we tend to cast ourselves in the role of victim and our partners in the role of villain . . ." (p. 24). From Andrew Christensen, Ph.D. & Neil S. Jacobson, Ph.D. (2000), *Reconcilable Differences* (New York: The Guilford Press).

[2]   "In the intricate reciprocity required for passionate intensity, each is both the victim of the other's insensitivity and cruelty and the intentional and unintentional agent of the other's pain. In prototypical couple arguments, both participants highlight their own victimization and minimize their own agency, elaborating self-pity and dodging guilt" (p. 154). From Mitchell (2002).

"Predatory partners also commonly feel like prey, and partners who feel like prey commonly act in a predatory manner" (p. 217). From Solomon & Tatkin (2011).

Chapter 6

[1]   Kaufman, Gershen. (1985). *Shame: The Power of Caring*, 2nd Ed. Cambridge, MA: Schenkman Books.

Morrison, Andrew P. (1989). *Shame: The Underside of Narcissism*. New York: Routledge.

NOTES

2   Cozolino (2006), p. 234.

Kaufman (1985) states that shame is induced by "breaking the interpersonal bridge" (p. 11).

3   Schore (1994).

Some psychologists have written that experiencing shame requires a more developed capacity for language and sense of self, and that therefore, as one of the "self-conscious" emotions, shame is not experienced until around 2–3 years of age. This is the position that Michael Lewis (2010) takes in his chapter, "Self-conscious emotions: Embarrassment, pride, shame, and guilt" (pp. 742–756), in Lewis, Haviland-Jones, & Barrett, Eds. (2010). An entirely different perspective is expressed by Colwyn Trevarthen in his chapter, "The functions of emotion in infancy: The regulation and communication of rhythm, sympathy, and meaning in human development" (pp. 55–85), in Fosha, Siegel, & Solomon, Eds. (2009). He states that shame can be experienced as early as six months of age (p. 79). I find the more valid position to be the one taken by several neuroscientists who believe that shame emerges in the first half of the second year of life when a child is beginning to experience mobility and independence and therefore to risk disapproval.

4   Cozolino (2006), pp. 233–235.

"(W)hen a child's desire to have his excited feelings mirrored is met with criticism, shame develops" (p. 75). From Shaddock (2005).

"At a moment of intensity, a failure to be understood, to be connected with emotionally, can result in a profound feeling of shame" (p. 275). From Siegel (2012).

5   Schore (1994), p. 244.

6   "(I)f the primary reason we select our mates is that they resemble our caretakers, it is inevitable that they are going to reinjure some very sensitive wounds" (p. 46). From Hendrix (1990).

Chapter 7

1   Many experts in couples therapy emphasize the cyclical nature of couples' problematic interactions:

Gerson (2010).

Greenberg & Goldman (2008).

Johnson & Denton (2002) in Gurman & Jacobson, Eds. (2002).

Nichols, Michael P. (2009). *Inside Family Therapy: A Case Study in Family Healing,* 2nd Ed. Boston: Pearson.

Shaddock (2005).

Solomon & Tatkin (2011).

Wile (2002) in Gurman & Jacobson, Eds. (2002).

2   Greenberg & Goldman (2008) write about "turning vicious cycles into virtuous ones" (p. 11).

Johnson & Denton (2002) in Gurman & Jacobson, Eds. (2002) state that couples can form "new cycles of emotional engagement and responsiveness" (p. 241).

"The good news is that committed partners with early attachment histories that are problematic can repair the past together" (p. 3). From Solomon & Tatkin (2011).

Daniel Wile (2002) in Gurman & Jacobson, Eds. (2002) writes that couples, "by discovering and confiding the 'leading-edge' thought or feeling of the moment . . . , can shift out of their withdrawn or adversarial cycle and into a collaborative one" (p. 281).

NOTES

[3]   "The lovers believe they are going to be healed—not by hard work or painful self-realization—but by the simple act of merging with someone the old brain has confused with their caretakers" (p. 52). From Hendrix (1990).

"What was unresolved was being replayed without conscious thought, with the hope that this time, what went wrong in childhood would be made right" (p. 247). From Solomon (2009) in Fosha, Siegel, & Solomon, Eds. (2009).

[4]   Freud described our attempts at "undoing what has been done" as a defense against loss and as the purpose for obsessional "repeating" (*The Standard Edition of the Complete Psychological Works of Sigmund Freud,* translated from the German under the general editorship of James Strachey, London: The Hogarth Press, 1958, Vol. 20, pp. 119–120), as quoted in Dayton (1997).

Chapter 8
[1]   Most authors who write about couple relationships emphasize the necessity of maintaining safety:

Greenberg & Goldman (2008).

Johnson (2008).

Shaddock (2005).

Solomon (2009) in Fosha, Siegel, & Solomon, Eds. (2009), p. 252.

Solomon & Tatkin (2011), p. xxi.

[2]   "(P)artners [must] still have an emotional investment in their relationship" (p. 233). From Johnson & Denton (2002) in Gurman & Jacobson, Eds. (2002).

[3]   Hendrix (1990).

        Shaddock (2005), p. 123.

[4]   Gottman & Silver (2000).

Chapter 9

[1]   Ogden (2009) in Fosha, Siegel, & Solomon, Eds. (2009), p. 229.

[2]   Brazelton & Cramer (1990).

        Cozolino (2006).

        Fosha, Siegel, & Solomon, Eds. (2009).

        Siegel (2012).

        Daniel Stern (1985) describes the importance of "the mutual exchange of social behaviors" between infants and parents (p. 43).

[3]   Bowen, Murray. (1978). *Family Therapy in Clinical Practice*. New York: Aronson.

        Gerson (2010).

        Nichols (2009).

        Shaddock (2005), p. 171.

[4]   Several experts on couples treatment refer to a "slowing down" that must happen to interrupt a recycling drama:

        Gerson (2010).

        Johnson & Denton (2002) in Gurman & Jacobson, Eds. (2002).

        Johnson (2008).

        Shaddock (2005).

        Solomon & Tatkin (2011) call for a similar type of "Holding and Waiting."

NOTES

5 "All courtship begins with a fantasy—a fervent desire, bordering on delusion, that another person can step in and magically undo all of life's hurts and disappointments. The new loved one will adore you forever, protect you, drive away wicked people, make you feel whole, valued, beautiful, worthy, and honorable—forever" (p. 38). From Wallerstein & Blakeslee (1996).

6 "The fact that many people find romantic excitement in a lover who displays the qualities of a rejecting parent, an excitement that they do not find in others, suggests the degree to which they remain not just committed to but enthralled by early attachment figures . . . It is as if they failed to mourn—not the death of a parent but rather the loss of a childhood they never had, happy and suffused with secure love" (p. 396). From Karen (1994).

7 "(E)motional needs for unconditional love, perfect understanding, large-scale nurturing, parental protection, and 'number one' status are doomed to frustration . . . While we can be cherished by our partners, being the be-all and end-all of their every waking moment is unlikely" (p. 198). From Piorkowski (1994).

8 With a mindset of "reciprocal discovery" (p. 300) and a "deep fascination with the personhood of the other" (p. 299), intimate partners should exercise "heightened curiosity in order to experience empathy and greater understanding . . . [of each other's] behavior" (p. 291). From Dan Hughes (2009), "The communication of emotions and the growth of autonomy and intimacy within family therapy" (pp. 280–303), in Fosha, Siegel, & Solomon, Eds. (2009). Dan further states, "Their curiosity about each other is not meant to control the other but rather to better know—and hopefully love—the other" (pp. 282–283).

In a repairing drama, "(t)he space opens up for curiosity, for reaching for the other's reality" (p. 137). From Johnson (2008).

[9]   "The overriding lesson is you have to take your partner's hurt seriously and hang in and ask questions until the meaning of an incident becomes clear, even if to you the event seems trivial or the hurt exaggerated" (p. 172). From Johnson (2008).

[10]   "We can have a clear sense that something happened when in fact it did not" (p. 66). From Siegel (2012).

Chapter 10

[1]   Diana Fosha (2009) writes about dealing with emotional pain as one of the essential steps in transformational experience (pp. 187–188). From Fosha, Siegel, & Solomon, Eds. (2009).

[2]   Couples "reexperience dysregulating affects in *affectively tolerable doses in the context of a safe environment, so that overwhelming traumatic feelings can be regulated and integrated*" (p. 130). From Schore (2009) in Fosha, Siegel, & Solomon, Eds. (2009).

"The . . . task is to create a compassionate perspective from which partners can empathize with each other about their interacting sensitivities—and about their uncomforted traumas, automatic incapacities, family-of-origin-based vulnerabilities, and moment-to-moment abandonments of each other. Everyone has had traumas that were never comforted. Being in a couple relationship provides the possibility for such comforting. [The] goal is to turn the relationship into a curative force" (p. 290). From Wile (2002) in Gurman & Jacobson, Eds. (2002).

[3]   Louis Cozolino (2006) clearly outlines how the neuroanatomy of anxiety and fear differ (pp. 247–251). He states that anxiety is the

result of "a lower level of diffuse arousal" than fear, and that anxiety creates "a sense of concern over a longer period of time" than fear (p. 248).

"'Fear' is said to differ from anxiety primarily in having an identifiable eliciting stimulus. In a sense, therefore, anxiety is often 'prestimulus' (i.e., anticipatory to [more or less real] threatening stimuli), whereas fear is 'poststimulus' (i.e., elicited by a defined fear stimulus)" (p. 710). From Arne Öhman (2010), "Fear and anxiety: Overlaps and dissociations" (pp. 709–729), in Lewis, Haviland-Jones, & Barrett, Eds. (2010). Öhman also points out that fear and anxiety are generated in different brain structures.

Chapter 11

1   Cozolino (2006), p. 250.

"(T)he first clear expressions of anger emerge at about 4 months of age, and ... anger expressions are targeted to a social figure by 7 months" (p. 731). From Elizabeth A. Lemerise & Kenneth A. Dodge (2010), "The development of anger and hostile interactions" (pp. 730–741), in Lewis, Haviland-Jones, & Barrett, Eds. (2010).

Panksepp (2009) in Fosha, Siegel, & Solomon, Eds. (2009).

2   "Survival considerations, either contemporary or in an evolutionary perspective, are relevant for most situational dimensions of human fears" (p. 711). From Öhman (2010) in Lewis, Haviland-Jones, & Barrett, Eds. (2010).

"(W)hen there is an obstacle to goal attainment, anger's function is to overcome obstacles in order to achieve goals" (p. 730). From Lemerise & Dodge (2010) in Lewis, Haviland-Jones, & Barrett, Eds. (2010).

Chapter 12

1   Shaddock, David. (2000). *Contexts and Connections: An*

Intersubjective Systems Approach to Couples Therapy. New York: Basic Books.

Siegel (2012), p. 328.

Chapter 13

[1]   "People need to be able to face their shame, rather than avoid it" (p. 24). From Greenberg & Goldman (2008).

"Shame in certain degrees is actually an essential emotion for children to experience, in order to begin to learn to self-regulate their state of mind and behavioral impulses" (p. 312). From Siegel (2012).

[2]   Shaddock (2005), p. 41.

Chapter 15

[1]   Bonanno, George A.; Goorin, Laura; & Coifman, Karin G. (2010). "Sadness and grief" (pp. 797–810), in Lewis, Haviland-Jones, & Barrett, Eds. (2010).

[2]   Dayton (1997).

Chapter 16

[1]   "Many spouses consider themselves far more mature than their partners, but in fact, when it comes to selecting mates, we tend to choose people who are at the same level of maturity, of emotional development, as our own" (p. 387). From Scarf (1988).

[2]   In Diana Fosha's chapter in Fosha, Siegel, & Solomon, Eds. (2009), she states that transformational experience leads to "the accessing of resources needed for the energetic pursuit of life: for growth, learning, and flourishing" (p. 201).

Daniel Siegel (2009, 2012) repeatedly refers to the freeing of energy for growth as an essential ingredient in the transformative process that he labels "integration."

3   "New thoughts, choices, and most importantly, new capacities arise spontaneously and lead to new pursuits and experiences . . . , which could have never been imagined" (p. 201). From Fosha (2009) in Fosha, Siegel, & Solomon, Eds. (2009).

4   "A good marriage, I have come to understand, is transformative. The prevailing psychological view has been that the central dimensions of personality are fully established in childhood. But from my observations, men and women come to adulthood unfinished, and over the course of a marriage they change each other profoundly" (p. 334). From Wallerstein & Blakeslee (1996).

5   "By dreams I mean the hopes, aspirations, and wishes that are part of your identity and give purpose and meaning to your life" (p. 218). From Gottman & Silver (2000).

"(W)hen [couples] can be engaged with, in contact with, and fully present to their experience—including the neglected emotions, felt meanings, and tacit knowing inherent in that experience—they can be creative, resourceful, and resilient" (p. 240). From Johnson & Denton (2002) in Gurman & Jacobson, Eds. (2002).

6   "(M)arriage can be the most therapeutic of relationships, the fertile terrain which permits both partners to expand, flourish and attain their full potentials" (p. 117). From Scarf (1988).

INDEX

INDEX

INDEX

relations, xv
Objective "truth", 80
Opposite, 69, 89, 94.
See also Dramas of opposites
    and Roles, Opposite
Overadapted, 126, 164
Overstimulated, xiii
Overstimulating, xiii

P
Panksepp, Jaak, 177
Parental, 36, 126-127
Parented, 164, 170
"Parentified child", 6
Parenting, xiii, xvii, 14, 164, 167
    deficiencies, 29, 40
Partnership, 166
    Adult, xvii, 108, 164
    Intimate, xvii, 108
Patterns
    Nonconscious, 13
    of interaction, ix, 11
    of relating, 1, 15, 17, 171
    Repetitive, 1
Perpetrator, 32, 70
Physiological, xviii
Power, xi, 12, 32, 36-37, 48, 71, 75,
    171, 177-179
Powerful, 10-12, 14, 30, 97, 170
Powerless, 30-31, 159
Powerlessness, 137-138

Psychodynamic, xviii, 178
Psychological, 31, 174-175, 178
    development, 62, 163
    growth and development,
        163-165
    matching, 61
    trauma, 177
Psychologists, 10
Psychology, 6, 16, 40, 73, 78, 163,
    174
    Developmental, 176
    of intimate relationships, xi,
        1, 173
    theory, xi, 173-179
Psychotherapists, 153
Psychotherapy, 178

R
Rage, 15, 23-24, 30-31, 39-40, 91,
    97-105, 143-144
Rational, xiii, 77
Reciprocal roles, see Roles,
    Reciprocal
Reciprocity, 6
Recognizing similarity, xvii, 17
Recycled, 25, 31, 84
Recycling, 71
    behavior, 77
    dramas, 51-63, 66-67, 70-71,
        74-77, 79-80, 84, 86, 88,
        90, 92-95, 98-100, 102,

Victims and villains dramas, 35-
40, 48, 88, 92, 109, 119,
139, 183

Villain, 31, 35-40, 66, 70-71, 91,
100, 110, 140, 144-147,
168, 183, 185

Violence, *see* Domestic violence

Vulnerability, xvii, 15, 66, 71

Vulnerable, xii, 65, 73, 154

W

Wall, Sally, 175

Waters, Everett, 175

Wile, Daniel, 179

Wound, 45, 56, 62, 74, 76, 83, 102,
119, 166

Wounded, 19, 45, 55, 118

Wounding, 19, 52, 85, 166

ABOUT THE AUTHOR

Jana Edwards, MSW, LCSW, has specialized in treating couples in her private practice in Denver, Colorado, for over thirty years. She has twice been named Most Distinguished Clinician by the Colorado Society for Clinical Social Work and recognized as a Master Scholar by the University of Denver Graduate School of Social Work. She teaches a course that she developed for couples therapists, entitled "Neurodynamic Couples Therapy," and she has presented papers at national and international conferences for mental health professionals.

Ms. Edwards has been married for thirty-three years and has two married stepchildren and five stepgrandchildren.